HABEAS CORPUS

A Play

by

ALAN BENNETT

SAMUEL FRENCH

LONDON

NEW YORK   TORONTO   SYDNEY   HOLLYWOOD

HABEAS CORPUS

Presented by Michael Codron in association with Stoll Productions at the Lyric Theatre, London, on May 10th, 1973, with the following cast of characters:

Arthur Wicksteed	Alec Guinness
Muriel Wicksteed	Margaret Courtenay
Dennis Wicksteed	Christopher Good
Constance Wicksteed	Phyllida Law
Mrs Swabb	Patricia Hayes
Canon Throbbing	Roddy Maude-Roxby
Lady Rumpers	Joan Sanderson
Felicity Rumpers	Madeline Smith
Mr Shanks	Andrew Sachs
Sir Percy Shorter	John Bird
Mr Purdue	Mike Carnell

The play directed by Ronald Eyre
Setting by Derek Cousins

The action takes place in and around the Wicksteeds' house in Hove

The play is divided into two Acts, the action being continuous

Time—the present

AUTHOR'S NOTE

The text printed here is as first performed at the Lyric Theatre, London, in May, 1973. In the rehearsal version of the play I included no stage directions in an effort to achieve as fluid a presentation as possible. In the printed version I have marked a minimum of entrances and exits to make the action more readily comprehensible to the reader.

The play was presented on an open stage furnished with three chairs. All props, telephone, parcel, etc., were handed in from the wings. Much of the dialogue was delivered straight to the audience to an extent that makes it tedious to indicate all remarks taken as asides.

I would like to thank Ronald Eyre for his invaluable assistance with the text.

ACT I

A bare stage, the only furnishings are three chairs
As the CURTAIN *rises, Dr Arthur Wicksteed enters*

Wicksteed Look at him. Just look at that look on his face. Do you know what that means? He wants me to tell him he's not going to die. You're not going to die. He is going to die. Not now, of course, but some time... ten, fifteen years, who knows? I don't. We don't want to lose you, do we? And off he goes. Sentence suspended. Another ten years. Another ten years showing the slides. "That's Malcolm, Pauline and Baby Jason." Another ten years going for little runs in the car. "That's us at the Safari Park." "So what did the doctor say, dear?" "Nothing, oh, nothing. It was all imagination." But it's not all imagination. Sometimes I'm afraid, it actually happens.

Mrs Wicksteed (*off*) Arthur! Arthur!

Wicksteed exits as Mrs Swabb enters from the opposite side with a vacuum cleaner

Mrs Swabb It's all in the mind. Me, I've never had a day's illness in my life. No. I tell a lie. I once had my tonsils out. I went in on the Monday; I had it done on the Tuesday; I was putting wallpaper up on the Wednesday. My name is Mrs Swabb (hoover, hoover, hoover) someone who comes in; and in all that passes, I represent ye working classes. Hoover, hoover, hoover. Hoover, hoover, hoover. Now then, let's have a little more light on the proceedings and meet our contestants, the wonderful, wonderful Wicksteed family.

Wicksteed enters, followed by Mrs Wicksteed (Muriel), Dennis and Constance

Eyes down first for tonight's hero, Dr Arthur Wicksteed, a general practitioner in Brighton's plush, silk stocking district of Hove. Is that right, Doctor?

Wicksteed Hove, that's right, yes.

Mrs Swabb And you are fifty-three years of age.

Wicksteed Dear God, am I?

Mrs Swabb I'm afraid that's what I've got down here.

Wicksteed Fifty-three!

Mrs Swabb Any hobbies?

Wicksteed No. No. Our friends, the ladies, of course, but nothing much else.

Mrs Swabb Do you mind telling us what your ambition is?

Wicksteed Ambition? No, never had any. Partly the trouble, you see. When you've gone through life stopping at every lamp-post, no time.

Mrs Swabb Next we have . . .

Mrs Wicksteed I can manage, thank you. Elocution was always my strong point. Speak clearly, speak firmly, speak now. Name: Wicksteed, Muriel Jane. Age? Well, if you said fifty you'd be in the target area. Wife to the said Arthur Wicksteed and golly, don't I know it. Still potty about him though, the dirty dog. Oh, shut up, Muriel.

Mrs Swabb And now—this is Dennis, only son of Arthur and Muriel Wicksteed. And what do you do, Dennis?

Dennis Nothing very much. I think I've got lockjaw.

Mrs Swabb Really? Whereabouts?

Dennis All over.

Mrs Swabb Are you interested in girls at all?

Dennis If they're clean.

Mrs Swabb That goes without saying. You don't want a dirty girl, do you?

Dennis In a way, I do, yes.

Mrs Wicksteed Dennis!

Mrs Swabb And now we have the doctor's sister, Miss Constance Wicksteed. Connie is a thirty-three-year-old spinster . . .

Connie I am not a spinster. I am unmarried.

Mrs Swabb And to go with her mud-coloured cardigan Connie has chosen a fetching number in form-fitting cretonne. Have you any boy friends, dear?

Connie No.

Mrs Swabb Connie, you big story! What about Canon Throbbing, our thrusting young vicar? Why! That sounds like his Biretta now.

Throbbing crosses the stage on his power-assisted bicycle and exits

Now, Connie, would you like to tell the Audience what your ambition is? Go on, just whisper.

Connie I'd like a big bust.

Mrs Swabb And what would you do with it when you'd got it?

Connie Flaunt it.

Mrs Wicksteed Connie!

Mrs Swabb Three strangers too are in the town. A lady and her daughter . . .

Sir Percy Shorter enters and pushes his way forward

Sir Percy Out of my way, we're wasting time: I am Sir Percy Shorter. Shorter, Percy, K.C.B., President, British Medical Association. Venuing this week at Brighton.

Mrs Wicksteed Percy!

Wicksteed My wife's sometime sweetheart.

Mrs Wicksteed The man I spurned.

Sir Percy Well? Aren't you going to ask me what my ambition is?

Mrs Swabb President of the British Medical Association! What more can a man want?

Sir Percy Revenge.

Mrs Swabb I don't like it. Two strangers now are in the town, a lady and her daughter . . .

Lady Rumpers appears

Lady Rumpers England, my poor England. What have they done to you? Don't touch me. That's one thing I've noticed returning to these shores. There's a great deal more touching going on. If I want to be touched I have people who love me who can touch me. Touching is what loved ones are for, because loving takes the sting out of it. Delia, Lady Rumpers, widow of General Sir Frederick Rumpers. Tiger to his friends and to his enemies too, by God. Does the name Rumpers ring a bell?

Wicksteed Very, very faintly.

Lady Rumpers Time was when it would have rung all the bells in England. Rumpers of Rhodesia, Rumpers of Rangoon—when the history of the decline of the British Empire comes to be written, the name Rumpers will be in the index. For many years we were stationed in Addis Ababa. Tiger was right-hand man to the Lion of Judah.

Mrs Swabb Haile Selassie.

Lady Rumpers There followed a short spell in K.L.

Mrs Swabb King's Langley.

Lady Rumpers Kuala Lumpur. Then we fetched up in Rhodesia. In a green meadow on the outskirts of Salisbury, roses bloom and the trees are alive with the songs of multi-coloured birds. There we laid him.

Dennis sniffs

I am upsetting you?

Connie He has hay fever.

Lady Rumpers From end to end I've searched the land looking for a place where England is still England.

Wicksteed And now she's hit on Hove.

Lady Rumpers My daughter Felicity . . .

Everyone looks but no-one enters

At present changing her Hammond Innes. We had a terrible experience coming down. We had to move our compartment three times to avoid a clergyman who was looking up her legs under cover of the *Daily Telegraph*

Mrs Wicksteed And such a respectable newspaper.

Lady Rumpers I lie awake at night in a cold sweat wondering what would happen if Felicity's body fell into the wrong hands.

Mrs Swabb But this is a doctor's. Doctors can touch anybody, because they don't have the feelings to go with it. That's what they go to medical school for.

Lady Rumpers Rubbish. Doctors are as bad as anyone else. I could tell you of a doctor who once touched me and I will never forget it.

Mrs Swabb There's no need to tell me, I know.

Mrs Wicksteed You know? How do you know?

Mrs Swabb Because I am Fate. I cut the string.
> I know all goings out and comings in.
> Naught escapes me in a month of Sundays:
> I know when they change their undies.
> Hoover, hoover, hoover.
> Hoover, hoover, hoover. (*She hands off the vacuum cleaner*)

All except Mrs Swabb exit

(*Moving the chairs*) Now a scene setting scene to set the scene and see the set, set the scene up and see the set up.

Wicksteed and Throbbing enter

Wicksteed A thorough examination? Are you ill?

Throbbing Never felt better. Your sister, Connie, and I are about to get married.

Wicksteed She hasn't told me.

Throbbing Probably because I haven't told her. But this is her last chance. Ten years of courtship is carrying celibacy to extremes.

Wicksteed Poor girl.

Throbbing And I thought before I embarked on the choppy waters of the *vita coniugalis* I'd better have the vessel overhauled. If I can stretch my metaphor.

Wicksteed Ah well, drop your trousers.

Throbbing What for?

Wicksteed The longer I practise medicine the more convinced I am there are only two types of cases: those that involve taking the trousers off and those that don't. I'm waiting.

Throbbing I'm a bit shy.

Wicksteed Why? No-one will come in.

Throbbing drops his trousers

Mrs Swabb instantly enters with her vacuum cleaner

Throbbing pulls up his trousers again

Mrs Swabb Hoover, hoover, hoover.

Wicksteed Get out.

Mrs Swabb Hoover, hoover, hoover.

Mrs Swabb exits

Throbbing Couldn't I go behind a screen?

Wicksteed In the course of thirty-odd years in pursuit of the profession of medicine, Canon Throbbing, a profession to which I unwittingly yoked myself in my callow youth, people have been taking their trousers off in front of me at the average rate of five times a day, five days a week, fifty-two weeks in the year. This means that at a conservative estimate and allowing for some duplication I have seen twenty-five thousand sets of private parts. The most conscientious whore could not have seen more. In the light of such statistics you are displaying not so much modesty as arrogance. TAKE THEM OFF.

Throbbing goes off

Wicksteed (*following him to the side of the stage*) We were taught many things at medical school, padre, but seeing through several thick layers of winceyette was not one of them.
Off.
Yes.
Turn round.
Bend over.
Got any feelings of nausea at all?
Throbbing (*off*) No.
Wicksteed Well God knows I do. It's all guesswork you know. I delve in their ears, I peer up their noses. I am glued to every orifice of the body like a parlour-maid at a keyhole.
Throbbing (*off*) May I get up now?
Wicksteed Shut up. And so it goes on. Day after day. Week after week. They troop in with their sore throats and their varicose veins. They parade before me bodies the colour of tripe and the texture of junket. Is this the image of God, this sagging parcel of vanilla blancmange hoisted day after day on to the consulting-room table? Is this the precious envelope of the soul? Is this . . .

Throbbing enters

Throbbing Is this on the National Health?
Wicksteed No. Why do you want to get married, anyway?
Throbbing Because—because I look up girls' legs.
Wicksteed Marriage won't stop that.
Throbbing Won't it?
Wicksteed I'm afraid not.
Throbbing You mean, you still do?
Wicksteed Me? No. I'm a doctor.
Throbbing Well, I do, and I'm a clergyman.
Wicksteed My poor sister. Because she's flat-chested he thinks she's religious.

Throbbing climbs on his bicycle and exits. Connie and Mrs Wicksteed enter

Connie I don't love him.

Mrs Wicksteed Love? You look on the shelf and you'll find it cluttered with dozens of spinsters gathering dust and all of them labelled "I was waiting for love". I married Arthur for love and what did I get? The mucky end of the stick. I could kick myself.

Wicksteed Do you know who I could have married?

Mrs Wicksteed Do you know who I could have married?

Wicksteed Sir Percy Shorter.

Mrs Wicksteed Sir Percy Shorter.

Wicksteed Twice the man Arthur ever was.

Mrs Wicksteed Twice the man Arthur ever was.

Wicksteed Or will be.

Mrs Wicksteed Or will be. I get to look more and more like the Queen Mother every day.

Dennis enters with a large book

Dennis Mother.

Mrs Wicksteed Yes?

Dennis I've got some bad news.

Mrs Wicksteed Yes?

Dennis I've only got three months to live.

Mrs Wicksteed Three months? Two months ago you only had ten days.

Dennis I made a mistake.

Mrs Wicksteed And what's happened to the galloping consumption you had last Thursday? Slowed down to a trot I suppose. What is it this time?

Dennis I've got a very rare disease.

Mrs Wicksteed You've got an extremely common disease. You've got a dose of the can't help its. You'd better ask your father.

Dennis He doesn't care.

Wicksteed That's true enough.

Dennis It's called Brett's Palsy. (*He shows her the medical book*)

Mrs Wicksteed (*reading*) Tiredness, irritability, spots, yes. And generally confined to the Caucasus. If this germ is confined to the Caucasus what's it doing in Hove?

Wicksteed Over here for the hols, I suppose.

Wicksteed exits

Mrs Wicksteed Tragic. And he came through puberty with such flying colours.

Mrs Wicksteed exits

Connie Every day and in every way they're getting bigger and bigger and bigger.

Dennis I'm going to die, Connie.

Connie Every day and in every way they're getting bigger and bigger and bigger.

Dennis I'm dying and no-one will believe me.

Mrs Swabb enters with a magazine and a postcard

Mrs Swabb Listen to this. "Lucille is from Sydenham. Her hobbies are water-skiing and world peace."

Dennis That's my magazine.

Mrs Swabb Someone hid it on top of the wardrobe.

Connie If I had those I wouldn't need hobbies.

Mrs Swabb No, dear. Look. "Send off this postcard and a beautiful bust can be yours this summer for only five pounds."

Dennis Two fifty each.

Connie False ones. Do you think so?

Dennis I would, Connie, if it were me.

Mrs Wicksteed enters

Mrs Wicksteed Connie? Connie? Who's Connie? I've told you before, Dennis. Connie has a title. She's your Aunt Connie.

Connie Aunt isn't a title.

Mrs Wicksteed It's the nearest you'll ever get to one. Calling your aunt by her Christian name. I knew a girl once who called her parents by their Christian names. She had a baby before she was seventeen. And what was the father called? She hadn't even bothered to ask. So much for names.

Mrs Wicksteed exits

Mrs Swabb fills in the postcard

Connie It's no use. Look at my legs.

Mrs Swabb Very nice legs, if you ask me. There are people running about with no legs at all, who'd be more than happy to have yours.

Connie By rights with me it ought to be all lemon tea and neutered cats. But it isn't. I look like this on the outside but inside I feel like Jan Masefield.

Mrs Swabb No, dear, Jayne Mansfield.

Connie No. Jan Masefield. She was a girl in the front row at my school. Actually it was the second row but it looked like the front row.

Mrs Swabb I'll post this postcard personally
    I'm sure it's for the best
    You wait she'll be a different girl
    With the Cairngorms on her chest.

Dennis Is that a lump there?

Connie Yes.

Dennis Oh God.

Connie Your fountain-pen. You want to say: look, this body doesn't really suit me. Could I move into something different? But you can't. The body's a tied cottage. At birth you're kitted out with mousey hair, bad legs, and no tits . . .

Mrs Swabb That's right, dear. You get it off your chest. Look out, it's the priest with five fingers.

Mrs Swabb exits

Throbbing enters

Throbbing Precious. Dr Wicksteed's given me a clean bill of health. Isn't it wonderful?
Dennis I've got Brett's Palsy.
Throbbing How interesting.
Dennis Three months to live.
Throbbing As long as that? It's the green light, Connie.
Dennis She hasn't said yes yet.
Throbbing With you sitting there she hasn't had much chance. Haven't you anything to do?
Dennis No.
Throbbing If I had only three months to live I'd have a hundred and one things to do.
Dennis Like what?
Throbbing Take my library books back, stop the papers, warn the milkman . . .
Dennis Death isn't like going away on holiday, you know.
Throbbing Oh yes it is. It's going away for a long, long holiday to a place by all accounts every bit as nice as Matlock. For some of us anyway.
Connie Dennis doesn't believe in heaven, do you, Dennis?
Dennis No. I don't know what it means.
Throbbing Nor did I till I met you, dearest. You'd better not sit near me. I've just been visiting the sick.
Connie Dennis!

Dennis exits hurriedly

Throbbing Alone at last.
Connie Yes.
Throbbing Just you and me.
Connie Yes.
Throbbing The two of us.
Connie Yes.
Throbbing How old are you, Connie?
Connie Thirty-three.
Throbbing What a coincidence.
Connie You're not thirty-three.

Throbbing No, but my inside leg is. Oh, Connie.
Connie Canon, please.
Throbbing Forgive me: I was carried away. Connie. Will you marry me?
  Will you marry me?

Mrs Swabb enters

Mrs Swabb Right now it's make up your mind time for thirty-three-year-
  old "I keep myself to myself" Connie Wicksteed, a spinster from
  Brighton's Hove. Does she accept the hand of slim, balding "Just pop
  this in your offertory box" Canon Throbbing, no dish it's true, but with
  a brilliant future on both sides of the grave
  or
  does she give him the elbow on the off-chance of something more
  fetching coming along once her appliance arrives?

Mrs Swabb exits

Connie Oh, Mr Right, where are you? Just give me a few more days.
  Until Thursday.

Wicksteed enters

Throbbing Very well. After all, what is two more days in Purgatory if it's
  followed by a lifetime in Paradise?

Connie exits followed by Throbbing

Wicksteed You silly man. You silly woman. Handcuffing yourselves together. Don't do it. What for? I'd rather have a decent glass of sherry
  any day. Of course, I despise the body. Despise it. Stroking faces, hold-
  ing hands, oh it all looks very nice on the surface, but look inside:
  the pipes are beginning to fur and the lungs to stiffen. We're all pigs,
  pigs; little trotters, little tails. Offal. Show me a human body and I will
  show you a cesspit.

Felicity enters in a pool of rosy light and to shimmering music

  I eat every word.
Felicity I was passing the door and I came over rather faint.
Wicksteed I feel just the same. Is there anything I could offer you?
Felicity If I could just sit down.
Wicksteed Perhaps you would like some tea—or would you prefer me to
  clap my moist lips over yours and plunge my tongue again and again
  into your mouth sending you mad with desire—or would you prefer
  coffee?
Felicity Anything.
Wicksteed What is your name?

Felicity Felicity.

Wicksteed Felicity what?

Felicity The Hon. Felicity Rumpers.

Wicksteed Indeed? Connie, fetch in the delphiniums will you: I think we have a private patient.

Felicity I'm feeling much better now.

Wicksteed Are you?

Felicity I like it here.

Wicksteed Yes?

Felicity The atmosphere. The feel of the place.

Wicksteed I'm glad. It's—it's a bit untidy. It could do with smartening up a bit. Old, I suppose, without being old-fashioned. Carpets a bit thin. Plumbing's a bit noisy sometimes too. Bit smelly, even. Tobacco. Drink. But I tell you: it's a good deal better than a lot of these cheap gim-crack things you could pick up these days, even if it is a bit run down.

Felicity Yes?

Wicksteed Yes.

The telephone rings. Wicksteed goes to the side and brings it on

Excuse me, Miss Rumpers, one moment. (*On the phone*) Hello. Dr Wicksteed's surgery. Wicksteed speaking. . . . Ah. Mr Purdue. . . . Yes. One moment. (*To Felicity*) This is an interesting call, Miss Rumpers, and one that illustrates how vital a part we doctors play in the community. I have always made a point of making myself available for anyone who cares to call, anyone in trouble, in despair, anyone in par-ticular who is contemplating suicide.

Felicity Suicide!

Wicksteed This patient, Mr Purdue, is on the brink of self-destruction. But before he actually attempts to take his own life, he calls me, his family doctor, knowing I will be here.

Felicity The poor man.

Wicksteed A kind voice, a friendly word will often just tip that delicate balance between life and death, will turn back the patient from embark-ing on that journey to that far country from whose bourne, as Shake-speare so well put it, no traveller returns. So if you'll excuse me, I'll just have a word with him—strictly speaking, of course, I shouldn't, as you're a private patient and he isn't. . . .

Felicity No, no, not at all.

Wicksteed That's most magnanimous of you.

Felicity No. I'm quite happy.

Wicksteed Well I only wish Mr Purdue was. (*On the phone*) Hello, Mr Purdue. Mr Purdue, hello. . . . He seems to have—hung up. I am won-dering whether I ought to give you a little examination.

Mrs Wicksteed (*off*) Arthur!

Wicksteed Though now would not appear to be the best time. Excuse me one moment.

Wicksteed exits

Felicity (*referring to her stomach*) It used to be so flat. Can you tell?
(*To the tune of "On the Isle of Capri"*)
T'was on the A forty-three that I met him.
We just had a day by the sea.
Now he's gone, and he's left me expecting.
Will somebody, please, marry me.

Dennis enters

Dennis I didn't know anyone was here.
Felicity Hello.
Dennis I've got a disease called Brett's Palsy. I've only got three months
to live.
Felicity Really?
Dennis Yes. At the outside.
Felicity But that's tragic.
Dennis I'm glad somebody thinks so.
Felicity You're so young.
Dennis Don't touch me. You're sure you haven't got any disease?
Felicity No, you have.
Dennis Yes, but I don't want any complications, do I?
Felicity You poor boy. Poor frightened boy.
Dennis Don't tell my father. He's a doctor.
Felicity Perhaps he could heal you.
Dennis Him? He couldn't heel a shoe.
Felicity This disease: you say there's no cure?
Dennis None.
Felicity And in three months you'll be dead?
Dennis I'm certain.
Felicity Look, I'd like to see you again. Can I?
Dennis Me? You must be peculiar.
Felicity I would, I would really.
Dennis When? I don't have much time.
Felicity Thursday two-thirty. Where?
Dennis Here.
Felicity My name's Felicity. What's yours?
Dennis Dennis.

Wicksteed enters

Wicksteed Trevor, what are you doing here. You've no business in the
consulting-room.
Dennis Good-bye, Penelope.
Felicity Felicity.
Dennis Yes.

Dennis exits

Wicksteed My son, I'm afraid. Trevor.

Felicity He said his name was Dennis.

Wicksteed Did he? Then it probably is. Look, the doctor-patient relationship is such an important one, one of mutual trust and respect. And here are you such a young, shy innocent creature and I'm— somewhat older. It would be helpful, I think, it would help me, if we could break the ice a bit and maybe perhaps sometime go for a spin in the car sometime, anytime, say Thursday at two-thirty?

Felicity My mother's very strict. I . . .

Wicksteed Splendid, I'll meet you at the end of the West Pier.

Mrs Wicksteed (*off*) Arthur!

Wicksteed You won't be late?

Felicity I'm never late.

Felicity exits

Wicksteed Coming, my love.
     No. Not too old at fifty-three.
     A worn defeated fool like me.
     Still the tickling lust devours
     Long stretches of my waking hours.
     Busty girls in flowered scanties
     Hitching down St Michael panties.
     Easing off their wet-look boots
     To step into their birthday suits.
     No! I am abusing my position
     As their trusty old physician.
     Virtue be mine, I will not do it
     Just to pacify this lump of suet.

Mrs Swabb looks round the corner of the proscenium arch

Mrs Swabb I see it all. His ruse I rumble:
     That spotless girl he means to tumble.

Mrs Swabb disappears. Mrs Wicksteed enters

Mrs Wicksteed Who was that?

Wicksteed Only a patient.

Mrs Wicksteed Man or woman.

Wicksteed They're all the same to me.

Mrs Wicksteed How old are we, Arthur?

Wicksteed You are fifty-one and I am . . .

Mrs Wicksteed Fifty-three.

Wicksteed Fifty-three. And it doesn't seem five minutes since I was sixteen.

Mrs Wicksteed When did the fire go out, Arthur?

Wicksteed What?

Mrs Wicksteed Nothing. It isn't as if he's attractive. I'm much more attractive than he is. If he would only stretch out his hand and say my name.

Wicksteed Muriel.

Mrs Wicksteed Yes.

Wicksteed It is your cake-decorating class on Thursday?

Mrs Wicksteed Yes. Why?

Wicksteed Then you won't be wanting the car.

Mrs Wicksteed No. Why?

Wicksteed I am going to the open session of the B.M.A. Conference.

Mrs Wicksteed Indeed? The house will be empty.

Wicksteed I'll put an end to this duplicity . . .
But not before I've had Felicity.
Then take, oh take this itch away
Lest my ruin end this play.

Wicksteed exits

The telephone rings

Mrs Swabb enters with the telephone and gives it to Mrs Wicksteed

Mrs Swabb Telephone. Telephone. Telephone.

Mrs Wicksteed Hello. Dr Wicksteed's residence. . . . Yes. Speaking. . . .
Percy!

Mrs Swabb That will be Sir Percy Shorter to whom some reference has already been made.

Mrs Swabb exits

Mrs Wicksteed After all these years! . . . Longing to. Longing to. . . .
Well, why not here? . . . Yes. Thursday afternoon. . . . No. He's going
out. . . . Yes. How exciting. . . . Yes. Mum's the word. Good-bye.
Kiss, Kiss, Kiss.

Mrs Wicksteed exits with the telephone. Mrs Swabb enters

Mrs Swabb (*picking up the magazine*) It is the afternoon of the Thursday
in question, and, lunch, cooked by the fair hands of guess who, is just
over. I started them off with a little clear soup with scattered *croûtons*,
followed by a fricassee of lamb with just a hint of rosemary. This I
garnished with diced carrots and pommes duchesses. Then they **had**
apple charlotte or the cheese board, followed by wafer thin mints and
a choice of beverages. I think they enjoyed it. (*She picks up the magazine*)

Wicksteed enters

Wicksteed It was disgusting.

Mrs Wicksteed enters. She is wearing a dashing hat with perky feathers

Mrs Wicksteed I think this hat suits me. Of course, it needs someone who can carry it off. You can't skulk about in a hat like this.

Connie enters in her cub mistress's uniform

Connie Has anyone seen my woggle?
Mrs Swabb When did you have it last?
Mrs Wicksteed I should look in what is inappropriately in your case called your breast pocket.
Mrs Swabb Here's another picture of Sir Percy addressing the conference.
Wicksteed He hasn't grown an inch in twenty years.
Mrs Wicksteed Size isn't everything.

Dennis enters

The door bell rings

Dennis (*aside*) She's early!
Mrs Wicksteed (*aside*) He's early!
Dennis ⎱
Mrs Wicksteed ⎰ I'll go. ⎨ (*Speaking together*)
Mrs Swabb Stand back! (*She goes to the side*) I am the door. It's not a person. It's a parcel. (*She takes a parcel on*)
Wicksteed A parcel?
Mrs Wicksteed A parcel!
Mrs Swabb A parcel! For Miss Wicksteed.
Connie For me?
Mrs Wicksteed Yes.
Connie I'm expecting it.
Mrs Wicksteed Who's it from?
Connie I don't know.
Mrs Wicksteed You're expecting it and you don't know who it's from? I've never heard of that before.
Wicksteed I have. My surgery's full of girls expecting something and they don't know who it's from.

Wicksteed exits

Mrs Wicksteed Most mysterious. Not that I'm in the least bit curious.

Mrs Wicksteed exits

Connie I think it's them.
Mrs Swabb Open it.
Connie I shan't dare wear them.
Mrs Swabb Come on.

Connie But it's time for cubs.

Mrs Wicksteed enters

Mrs Wicksteed Mrs Swabb, you may take the afternoon off.

Mrs Swabb But I have an enormous backlog of dusting.

Mrs Wicksteed I insist—all work and no play makes Jack a dull boy. And talking of dull boys, what are your plans?

Dennis A long walk in the fresh air.

Mrs Wicksteed Splendid. And you?

Connie Cubs. Why?

Mrs Wicksteed Just asking. I'm going to my cake-decorating class. I don't really want to, but we're electing a new secretary and it's like anything else: if the rank and file don't go the militants take over.

Mrs Wicksteed exits

They open the parcel

Mrs Swabb "I was a spinster for fifteen years", writes Miss P.D. of Carshalton. "Three years ago I invested in your appliance, and since then I have been engaged four times."

Dennis "The Rubens, in sensitized Fablon, as used on Apollo space missions." Try it on.

Connie No. It's too late.

Mrs Swabb It's never too late. Listen. "In reply to yours . . . Etc., etc. They are easily fitted without assistance but to forestall any difficulties our fitter Mr Shanks will call on Thursday May twenty-ninth."

Dennis That's today.

Connie But he can't. I'm not here. I'm at cubs.

Mrs Wicksteed, off, claps her hands

Mrs Swabb Look out. Heads down.

Connie What shall I do?

Mrs Wicksteed enters

Mrs Swabb Say you're ill.

Mrs Wicksteed Still hanging about? You should have been at the toadstool half an hour ago! A scout is punctual at all times. That was the rule when I was a scout.

Dennis She's ill.

Mrs Wicksteed She's late. Come along, clear the decks.

Wicksteed enters

Off, off, off. Out, out, out. Good-bye, house, good-bye, chairs—good-bye.

Wicksteed What's all the hurry? Anybody'd think you wanted us out of the way.

Mrs Wicksteed Wanted you out of the way? What a ridiculous idea! What an absurd idea! Why, the idea is absurd. It is ridiculous. Relax. There's plenty of time. It's only two-thirty.

Wicksteed Two-thirty. My God! Two-thirty. Plenty of time! Don't be ridiculous. There's not a moment to lose.

Wicksteed exits. Mrs Wicksteed, Dennis and Connie follow

Mrs Swabb Quiet, isn't it? It won't last. Give them five minutes and they'll be in and out of here like dogs at a bazaar. Sniffety, sniffety, sniff. On the fruitless pursuit of bodily pleasures. Oh, it's all such a waste of time. After all, as I tell my husband, what is the body but the purse of the soul? What is the flesh but the vest of the spirit? Me, I don't bother with sex. I leave that to the experts.

Mrs Swabb exits. Dennis and Felicity enter

Dennis Hello.
Felicity Hello, Dennis.
Dennis You remembered my name, Penelope.
Felicity Felicity.
Dennis I'm supposed to be out for a long walk.
Felicity I'm supposed to be meeting your father. What are you staring at?
Dennis Nothing. You.
Felicity Me? What for?
Dennis You're so nice looking, firm and full whereas . . .
Felicity Your poor hands. All those long, thin fingers.
Dennis See all the veins. Horrible.
Felicity I don't mind.
Dennis Don't you honestly?
Felicity Girls don't. They don't expect all that much. That's the first lesson you've got to learn. Most men don't bear close examination.
Dennis You seem to know a lot about it. I know nothing. I've got such a lot to learn.
Felicity And so little time to learn it.
Dennis And nobody to teach me. I was wondering . . .
Felicity Yes?
Dennis Could we go for a walk?
Felicity It's too hot for walking.
Dennis Yes. I suppose it is.
Felicity Of course, we could walk a little—then throw ourselves down in some lush warm summer-scented meadow.
Dennis I get hay fever.
Felicity Or pause by a sparkling stream and perch together on some cool, moss-grown rock.
Dennis I get piles.
Felicity Nature is hard.

Dennis I could take my raincoat.
Felicity What a brilliant idea.
Dennis Felicity.
Felicity What?
Dennis I feel very peculiar. I think I may be catching something.

Dennis and Felicity take hands and go. Mrs Swabb enters, with a copy of the "Lancet"

Mrs Swabb Bless them! I think they've clicked. Scorpio and Sagittarius. Lovely combo. Well, I think I'll just have a glance at the *Lancet*.

Mrs Wicksteed enters

Mrs Wicksteed You!
Mrs Swabb The mistress of the house! I wasn't expecting your return.
Mrs Wicksteed No, I have returned unexpectedly. An unforeseen hitch at my cake-decorating class! A shortage of hundreds and thousands put paid to the proceedings. Anyway, I thought I gave you the afternoon off.
Mrs Swabb I am an indefatigable worker.
Mrs Wicksteed You are a Nosey Parker. If you're so anxious to be doing something, there's one or two groceries waiting to be picked up.
Mrs Swabb Where?
Mrs Wicksteed Sainsbury's, where else? That takes care of her for the next two hours.

Mrs Wicksteed and Mrs Swabb exit

Sea sounds

Wicksteed enters

Wicksteed (*alone*) Break, break, break
    On the cold grey stones, O Sea
    And would that my tongue could utter
    The thoughts that arise in me.
Would that it could, but you see, Felicity, I'm rather a shy person.
Are you, Doctor?
Don't call me Doctor. Call me Arthur.
Are you, Arthur?
Now you mention it, Felicity, I suppose I am. But you, Felicity—you somehow restore my faith in human kind, remind me of what perfection the human body is capable. And spirit, oh yes, and spirit, Felicity. To think I was already qualified when you were born. I might have brought you into the world, felt the first flutter of your fragrant life. I could have cradled you in my arms, touched your little face . . .
Arthur.

Yes, Felicity?
Arthur, you could still.
Could I? Oh, Felicity.

Wicksteed exits

The door bell rings

*Mrs Wicksteed and Mr Shanks enter from opposite sides. He has a
Polaroid camera*

Mrs Wicksteed Percy . . . Oh, good afternoon.

Shanks I'm looking for someone by the name of Wicksteed. W-I-C-K-
S-T-E-E-D. Wicksteed. Yes.

Mrs Wicksteed Yes?

Shanks And I think I've found her. Shanks is the name. Full marks. Ten
out of ten. They are wonderful. *Wonderful.*

Mrs Wicksteed You think so?

Shanks They are outstanding. Out-standing.

Mrs Wicksteed Golly. Appreciation after all these years.

Shanks What a charming home, and my goodness, don't they enhance
it. The balance, dear lady, almost perfect. Almost, but not quite. Still,
that's what I'm here for. May I?

Mrs Wicksteed This is what they must mean by the Permissive Society.

Shanks I believe this one is a fraction bigger than the other.

Mrs Wicksteed To hell with symmetry. How that touch revives me.

Shanks It will not have escaped your notice that the customer, Miss
Wicksteed, is becoming a little excited.

Mrs Wicksteed At last! A tenant for my fallow loins.

Shanks However, rest assured. This excitement is not mutual. I am an
expert. A crash course at Leatherhead, the firm's training centre, set
in the heart of Surrey's famous rural surroundings, lays down a stan-
dard procedure for every eventuality. Mind you, these are exceptional.
I've only seen one pair to rival these, and she's now the manageress of
the only cinema in Fleetwood. Look, you're such an outstanding example, we often compare notes, my colleagues and I—and since I've
got my little Polaroid handy . . .

Mrs Wicksteed I was wondering when you were going to mention that.
Your Polaroid, your lovely little Polaroid . . .

Shanks Some snaps—just for the record . . .

Mrs Wicksteed Yes, yes, a record. Music!

The stage is flooded with sensual music

Muriel Wicksteed, what are you doing? (*Dancing and posing while he
snaps her*) Can this be you? Yes. Yes, it is me. The real me. The me
I've always been deep down. Suddenly the body reasserts itself, breaks
through the dead crust of morality, and from the chrysalis convention
bursts the butterfly, freedom.

The telephone rings

I will see to that. (*She goes and fetches the telephone. On the telephone*) Dr Wicksteed's residence.... Oh, it's you, Mr Purdue.... No, you cannot speak to Dr Wicksteed. This is his afternoon off.... You're about to commit suicide? I see. If you must choose to commit suicide on doctor's afternoon off, that's your funeral. *Au revoir*. Or I suppose I should say good-bye. (*She replaces the receiver and hands the telephone off*) Now where was I ... Oh yes. (*She embraces Shanks*)

Shanks I repeat, there is nothing to be ashamed of. This is all in a day's work to me.

Mrs Wicksteed I don't think he should throw his promiscuity in my face. One doesn't like to think one is simply a convenience.

Shanks A client not a convenience.

Mrs Wicksteed Client? I'm not going to have to pay you for this?

Shanks It's all included in the five pounds.

Mrs Wicksteed Five pounds! That's wicked.

Shanks There's nothing more I can do.

Mrs Wicksteed He comes in here, goes for my bust like a bull at a gate and then says there's nothing more he can do. There is more. "The bust is but the first port of call on the long voyage of love."

Shanks I have other ladies to see.

Mrs Wicksteed Other ladies. The idea!

Shanks Stop. Take them off. They are a sacred trust. You are not fit to wear them. (*He slaps her bust*)

Shanks It's the—it's the real thing, isn't it? Flesh.

Mrs Wicksteed Of course it's flesh. What did you think it was—blanc-mange?

Shanks Is there anywhere I could wash my hands?

Mrs Wicksteed Time enough to wash your hands when we've been to Paradise and back.

Shanks No!

Mrs Wicksteed No. That means yes. So much at least Freud has taught us.

Mrs Wicksteed drags Shanks off

Sea sounds

Wicksteed enters

Wicksteed It shocks you, I'm afraid, me a respectable, middle-aged doctor waiting like a fool on the end of Brighton Pier. Ludicrous? But listen.

Say nobody saw and nobody heard
Say no-one at all would breathe a word
Say nobody knew the you that was you
And your secret dreams could all come true.
Picture the scene, figurez-vous,

You could have whoever you wanted to:
Felicity Rumpers, Omar Sharif,
Julie Andrews, Mr Heath.
Orgies of swapping, five in a bed.
You, me and Omar, Julie and Ted.
Don't tell me you wouldn't, given the choice
Old men with schoolgirls, ladies with boys
If she's what I fancy you really can't quarrel,
'Cos given the chance you'd be just as immoral.
Nobody's perfect: I'm fifty-three.
And the tide's going out, Arthur Wicksteed, M.D.

Wicksteed exits. Shanks enters from the opposite side, pursued by Mrs Wicksteed

Shanks No, no, please, no.

Mrs Wicksteed I am Diana. You are my quarry. I am stalking you with all the lithe grace of a panther.

Shanks Does anyone know the dialling code for Leatherhead?

Mrs Wicksteed I close in for the kill, my haunches taut, my flanks rippling . . .

Shanks No, no.

Mrs Wicksteed My head goes down and I pounce.

Sir Percy enters

Shanks Yee-ow.

Shanks makes a run for it, straight into the arms of Sir Percy

Sir Percy I'm looking for Mrs Wicksteed.

Mrs Wicksteed Percy! Don't you recognize me?

Sir Percy Muriel. You haven't changed. She's enormous.

Mrs Wicksteed Do you know each other?

Sir Percy No.

Shanks How do you do.

Sir Percy How do you do. I was wondering whether. . . . } (*Speaking*
Mrs Wicksteed I suppose I ought to . . .   } *together*)

Sir Percy Perhaps you would tell me . . .
Mrs Wicksteed In case you're wondering . . . } (*Speaking together*)

Shanks Er . . .

Sir Percy Yes?

Shanks Nothing.

Sir Percy Muriel, this man isn't your husband?

Mrs Wicksteed Yes! No.

Sir Percy Ah. I saw no resemblance but twenty years is a long time.

Mrs Wicksteed It is, it is.

Sir Percy If he is not your husband, what is he doing in his shirt tails?

Mrs Wicksteed He's a patient.

Sir Percy A patient.
Mrs Wicksteed What did you think he was—my lover? Ha, ha, ha, ha, ha.
Sir Percy Ha, ha, ha, ha, ha.
Shanks Ha, ha, ha, ha, ha.
Sir Percy What are you laughing at? You've got no trousers on.
Shanks I can explain that.
Sir Percy Did anyone ask you?
Shanks No.
Sir Percy Are you a private patient?
Shanks No.
Sir Percy Then shut up. Unbalanced?
Mrs Wicksteed Mad. He only called for his tranquillizers.
Sir Percy Don't worry. I have some with me.
Shanks You have to padlock your underpants when she's around, I can
tell you.
Sir Percy Really?
Shanks She's man mad.
Mrs Wicksteed Me. Ha. She laughed her scornful laugh.
Sir Percy Here, take these.
Shanks No.
Sir Percy I am President of the British Medical Association. Take them.

Mrs Wicksteed goes off and returns with a hypodermic

Shanks No.
Sir Percy Very well. Muriel, we must go intravenous.

Mrs Wicksteed prepares the hypodermic

Shanks She took my trousers off.
Sir Percy What for?
Shanks What for? What do people usually take other people's trousers
off for?
Sir Percy You tell me.
Shanks She wanted my body.
Sir Percy Your body. Your body? Thank you, Muriel. In case of doubt,
just knock them out.
Shanks What?
Sir Percy When hackles rise, I tranquillize. (*He bends Shanks over*)
Mrs Wicksteed They do less harm if you keep them calm.
Sir Percy Hold him, Muriel.
Shanks No. No. All I want is to telephone Leatherhead.

Sir Percy injects him

Sir Percy This is the way we generally telephone Leatherhead. That's it.
Up you get.
Shanks Please. Does anyone know the dialling code for Leatherhead?

Shanks collapses

Sir Percy Typical of your husband.

Mrs Wicksteed Arthur?

Sir Percy Leaving a patient running loose about the place.

Mrs Wicksteed It wasn't really his fault.

Sir Percy Slapdash. Inconsiderate. Don't suppose he's changed.

Mrs Wicksteed You haven't changed either. Have I?

Sir Percy I never liked him. He once said I was small. You were a fool, Muriel.

Mrs Wicksteed What?

Sir Percy To throw yourself away on that little nobody. Still, I suppose he makes you happy.

Mrs Wicksteed Arthur? He falls asleep as soon as his teeth hit the glass. Oh Percy.

Sir Percy Is he about, your husband? I'd quite like to see him. The years have doubtless taken their toll?

Mrs Wicksteed No. He's gone to the conference. The open session.

Sir Percy What open session? There is no open session today.

Mrs Wicksteed You're certain?

Sir Percy Of course. I am the President. How else could I be here.

Mrs Swabb enters with a wheeled basket of groceries

Mrs Wicksteed You've been quick.

Mrs Swabb I had a following wind.

Mrs Wicksteed Where is Dr Wicksteed?

Mrs Swabb Dr Wicksteed? He's on the Pier.

Mrs Swabb exits

Mrs Wicksteed I fear the worst.

Sir Percy Death?

Mrs Wicksteed Sex. And if I know him, he's with a patient.

Sir Percy A patient? Indeed! First item on the agenda—get your things on. Second, a visit to the Pier. Come on, buck up. And third, the ruin of a certain general practitioner.

He lifts the semi-conscious Shanks, who hangs like a dummy in his arms

Take careful note of all you see.

Mrs Wicksteed I will, I will, and who knows . . .

Sir Percy Yes?

Mrs Wicksteed This may be a blessing in disguise.

Shanks Disguise.

Mrs Wicksteed I shall be free.

Shanks Free.

Mrs Wicksteed And together the future will be ours.

Mrs Wicksteed exits

Shanks Ours.
Sir Percy No fear. But revenge, ha, ha.
Shanks Ha, ha.
Sir Percy After all these years.
Shanks All these years.
Sir Percy I think we need a booster.
Shanks Booster.

Sir Percy exits carrying Shanks

Sea sounds

Wicksteed enters

Wicksteed As the sun went down on that long afternoon, a lean, distinguished figure might have been observed standing all of an hour at the end of the Pier. Several times he made as if to greet solitary ladies as they approached, but each time he fell back, disappointed and alone.

Wicksteed exits. Sir Percy and Mrs Swabbs enter, meeting

Mrs Swabb Ah, I know who this is. Mr Shanks. I'll call her down, Mr Shanks. She's upstairs. Miss Wicksteed, your visitor.

Connie enters, wearing her appliance. Mrs Swabb exits

Connie Well? What do you think of them? Aren't they wonderful.
Sir Percy This must be what they mean by the Permissive Society.
Connie They've been held up by the rail strike.
Sir Percy Is that what it is? You *are* Miss Wicksteed, aren't you?
Connie Yes, why?
Sir Percy Her boldness rouses me strangely.
Connie Touch them if you like, they're very firm. But I suppose you know that.

Sir Percy touches her. His trousers fall

I don't think you ought to get excited.
Sir Percy No?
Connie Tell me, if someone were stroking them would they be able to tell the difference?
Sir Percy I don't follow.
Connie Would they be satisfied?
Sir Percy In due course, I hope, yes. Suspenders, Miss Wicksteed, how nice to find someone keeping up with the old ways. Oh God, think of all the years I've wasted. This is the sort of woman I've been waiting for. Bold, provocative with an ardour equal to mine. Come, let me clasp your urgent young body. Kiss me. Again. You earth maiden, will you marry me?

Connie And I've only had them on five minutes! This is what they must mean by the Permissive Society. Could I ask you something?
Sir Percy Yes.
Connie Are you supposed to wash them?
Sir Percy You mean, you don't?
Connie No. Not yet.
Sir Percy You mad Lawrentian Creature.
Connie I'd thought of brushing them. I've got a wire brush that might do.

Connie leads Sir Percy off. Throbbing enters

Throbbing Ah, a pair of trousers. Oxfam! Zambia will be so grateful.

Connie and Sir Percy enter, tangoing across the stage, and exit

Throbbing But what is this? My bride to be in the arms of another man, and before we're even married.

Connie and Sir Percy return, still tangoing, Connie leaves Sir Percy and joins Throbbing at the end of the dance

Connie My fiancé. (*She faints*)
Sir Percy She has fainted. Stand back. I am a doctor.
Throbbing You don't look like a doctor to me. You haven't any trousers on. You look like a cad and a loose fish. Get away, bending over the prostrate body of my fiancée in your underclothes, that is my privilege.
Sir Percy Poor fool. She thought she could seduce me.
Throbbing Seduce? Her? I have been engaged to Miss Wicksteed for ten years and she has never so much as laid a finger on me.
Sir Percy King Sex is a wayward monarch.
Throbbing Come on, come on. Stand up and fight. Stand up.
Sir Percy I am standing up.
Throbbing You'll probably want some handicap on account of your size.
Sir Percy What did you say?
Throbbing I'm bigger than you are.
Sir Percy What gives you that idea?
Throbbing One doesn't exactly have to be a quantity surveyor. Little squirt.
Sir Percy (*as he lands a blow*) LITTLE!
Throbbing Ooh! Ahh! Look. Can't we just talk this over? I've known quite a lot of small people in my time.
Sir Percy Small? Small?
Throbbing I don't hold anybody's size against them. We don't know how big Shakespeare was, do we? And look at Hitler. Mind you, he's a bad example. Connie, are you all right?
Connie Yes.
Throbbing Has this man been interfering with you?
Connie Yes. Yes, oh yes. I'm going to marry him.

Throbbing *Him?*
Sir Percy Why not, sailor?
Connie Yes, why not? He found in me something I never knew was there.
Throbbing Connie. What are those?
Connie They're a recent development.
Throbbing What is his name?
Connie I haven't asked.
Throbbing You're going to marry him and you don't even know his name?
Connie Yes, I do know his name. His name is curtains billowing wide on a summer night. His name is a special secret rose pressed in an old book. His name is the name of all lovers down the ages who have cried their challenge to the wild night and dared to cast themselves away on the frail bark of love. What is your name, by the way?
Sir Percy Sir Percy Shorter.

Connie screams and exits

It's not my fault if I send women mad.
Throbbing Mad? You? You Mickey Mouse. Why don't you marry some-one your own size? Goodness! It's time for Evensong.
Sir Percy That settles it. You're a clergyman. Start saying your prayers!

Dennis and Felicity come in with Mrs Swabb

Mrs Swabb Canon Throbbing, I don't think you know Miss Rumpers, newly returned from Addis Ababa.
Throbbing Welcome to our shores.

Mrs Swabb exits

Sir Percy primes his hypodermic

Felicity What are you doing?
Sir Percy The balance of his mind is disturbed. I am about to redress it.

Throbbing exits, pursued by Sir Percy

Felicity How do you think it will happen, then?
Dennis I imagine you just sort of fade away really. Don't let's talk about it.
Felicity How tragic. A widow at twenty-two.
Dennis I don't want to think about it any more.
Felicity No. I too will be brave. I will be more than brave. I will be plucky. "Felicity, his plucky young wife, survives him."
Dennis All the germs will flee before the greatest medicine of them all.
Felicity Love?

Dennis Sex.

To the tune of "Shuffle off to Buffalo"

> We've been going rather steady
> So it's time to go to beddy
> Turn the lights down low.

Felicity Oh, oh, oh.

Dennis You know which way we're heading
> We're heading for a wedding.

Mrs Swabb enters

Mrs Swabb Oh no, no, no, no, NO?

Dennis ⎱ "Some day the stork will pay a visit ⎰
Mrs Swabb ⎰ and leave a little souvenir.   ⎱ *(Singing together)*

Dennis Just a little cute what is it.

Felicity We'll discuss that later, dear."

Dennis You go home and get your knickers
> And I'll race you to the vicar's
> And it's ends away.

Felicity ⎱
Dennis ⎰ Mm, mm, mm. ⎰ *(Singing together)*

Mrs Swabb Don't anticipate it
> Wait to consummate it
> Not every day's a wedding day.

Mrs Swabb exits

Dennis kisses Felicity passionately

Dennis You put your tongue in my mouth. Are you supposed to do that?

Felicity It's optional.

Dennis This is what they must mean by the Permissive Society. Penelope.

Felicity Felicity.

Wicksteed enters

Wicksteed Ah! Is this your long walk in the fresh air?

Dennis It's all right.

Wicksteed All right? You lay your acned face in Miss Rumpers' lap—good afternoon, Miss Rumpers—and you say it's all right.

Dennis She doesn't mind. It's mutual.

Wicksteed Mutual! HA! It is never mutual. Get off. Get off. Be careful, I implore you, Miss Rumpers. That head is riddled with dandruff. Get out, you lounge lizard. You're not fit to hold a candle to Miss Rumpers, let alone anything else.

Dennis exits

My dear young lady, how can you forgive me? In my own house ...
Felicity Dennis and I——
Wicksteed Stop! Stop! Do not couple your name with his. That he should even contemplate touching your fresh, clean, innocent, young body fills me with such shame, such loathing. Filth, filth. Forgive me. (*He raises his hand to her shoulder*)
Felicity No! Do not touch me.
Wicksteed No. How can I approach you? How can I even speak to you? The least thing about you, the spent cartridge of your lipstick, the dry bed of your compact, the fluff in your handbag's bottom, all the fragrant clutter of your loveliness, I am as dirt and vileness beside it. But ...
Felicity But?
Wicksteed But speaking thus I speak as a man. And as a man I cannot touch you, but as a doctor ...
Felicity Does that make a difference?
Wicksteed Oh yes. As a man I see you as a fresh, lovely, passionate creature. As a doctor, you are to me a machine, an organism, a mere carcass. Feeling does not enter into it. As a doctor I am a eunuch: I touch you—without passion, and without desire. (*He puts his arm around her shoulder*)
Felicity Yes.
Wicksteed Now I touch you as a man.
Felicity Yes.
Wicksteed Now I touch you as a doctor.
Felicity Yes.
Wicksteed You feel the difference? So have no fears, my dear young lady, when in a few moments I shall ask you to remove your clothes in their entirety. Because I shall be as far from desire as is a plumber uncovering a manhole. Off. Off.

Felicity goes off

(*Following her to the side of the stage*) How well I understand your fears. Life is such a dirty business these days. Everyone trying to grab what he can. What is the poem ...
Felicity (*off*) I don't know.
Wicksteed A young Diana golden haired,
Stands dreaming on the verge of strife,
Magnificently unprepared.
For the long littleness of life.
Are you prepared for that, Felicity?
The long littleness—sometimes longer, sometimes littler
It comes as quite a shock to some girls ... others just take it in their stride.

Felicity enters in her slip

Hello. (*He kisses her*)

Hello, ears.
Hello, eyes.
Hello, nose.
Hello, mouth.
Hello, fingers.

Sir Percy enters and watches aghast

Hello, knees.
Hello, Percy.

Sir Percy So.

Wicksteed I was just giving this young lady an aspirin.

Sir Percy In her underclothes?

Felicity It's very hot in here.

Wicksteed Don't worry. I have a diploma in tropical medicine. Felicity, Miss Rumpers, I don't think you know Sir Percy Shorter.

Wicksteed ⎫
Sir Percy ⎬ President of the British Medical Association. ⎰ *(Speaking*
                                                            ⎱ *together)*

Sir Percy Is this young lady a patient of yours?

Wicksteed The idea that a doctor of my reputation would meddle with a patient is repugnant to me. Leave my ears alone will you, dear. And if not a patient, what?

Sir Percy You tell me.

Felicity goes behind Wicksteed and puts her hands in his trouser pockets

Wicksteed A friend. Of the family. The whole family. Like you. Strange, because she's not a bit like you. Come out of there, Miss Rumpers. Nothing in my trousers pocket of any interest to you. Humbugs, you know. She knows I keep them there.

Sir Percy You're old enough to be her father.

Wicksteed So are you.

Sir Percy She wasn't tickling my ears.

Wicksteed That's true, Miss Rumpers, why don't you tickle Percy's ears. I don't think she wants to. I'm not surprised.

Sir Percy Enough of this. Shall I tell you what I think?

Wicksteed No.

Felicity Yes.

Sir Percy I think this young woman is a patient. That you were abusing your position to interfere with her. That it is a scandal. That you are a blackguard. That it is my duty to bring your little games to the notice of the Medical Disciplinary Committee. That I will do all in my power to have you struck off.

Wicksteed No.

Sir Percy What have you to say to that?

Wicksteed You little pratt.

Sir Percy WHO ARE YOU CALLING LITTLE?

Mrs Wicksteed enters

Mrs Wicksteed Arthur!

Wicksteed Muriel!

Sir Percy I have just discovered your husband with his tongue down this young lady's throat.

Mrs Wicksteed Kissing. Kissing. You slut!

Sir Percy I fear kissing was just the tip of the iceberg.

Mrs Wicksteed Of course I've known for years our marriage has been a mockery. My body lying there night after night in the wasted moonlight. I know now how the Taj Mahal must feel.

Wicksteed Listen. I can explain everything.

Mrs Wicksteed No. Save it for the decree nisi.

Wicksteed Divorce? We can't get divorced. Think of our son, Trevor— Keith . . .

Mrs Wicksteed DENNIS.

Wicksteed He will be the child of a broken home. He will probably turn to juvenile delinquency.

Mrs Wicksteed He is too old for juvenile delinquency.

Wicksteed Thank God for that.

Mrs Wicksteed Mention of divorce and avenues open up all round. Think of it, Percy: a hostess, perhaps at one of our leading London hotels, catering for an international clientele, where my knowledge of languages can be put to good use.

Wicksteed You have no knowledge of languages.

Mrs Wicksteed A smile knows no frontiers. Thank goodness I'm not alone.

Wicksteed And now, suddenly, at this moment of rejection, she goes knock, knock, knock at the door of my heart, and through a gap in the chintz I see the ghost of an old passion.

Sir Percy Come, Muriel, lean on me.

Purdue enters with a ready-noosed rope

Purdue Excuse me, Doctor . . .

Wicksteed I'm sorry, Mr Purdue. It's my afternoon off. I have lost my career. I have lost my wife. You are all I've got left.

Felicity Me?

Wicksteed Yes. But we can be happy together, you and I. Together we can defy the world. Snap our fingers at public opinion. What do you say, Felicity?

Purdue is meanwhile preparing to hang himself

Dennis enters

Dennis Can I help, Mr Purdue?

Purdue Nobody can help me.

Dennis Oh, don't say that.

Sir Percy I won't mention my engagement for the moment. She'll understand, of course. Sensible girl. Never been the clinging type.

Purdue I'm going to do it. (*He climbs on a chair*)

Mrs Wicksteed Come, Percy. Come into the house of my body. Shelter from the storms of life under the eaves of my breasts.

Purdue I am going to do it.

Wicksteed What do you say?

Felicity Actually, I'm already spoken for.

Wicksteed Spoken for? By whom?

Felicity Dennis.

Wicksteed Dennis? Who's Dennis?

Felicity Your son, Dennis.

Dennis and Felicity embrace

Wicksteed Leonard! O my God!

Purdue I'm going to do it. I am really.

Mrs Wicksteed What are you doing standing on my best chair?

Purdue Oh, sorry.

Mrs Wicksteed removes the chair, leaving Purdue hanging. Dennis and Felicity are clasped in each other's arms

Mrs Swabb enters followed by Lady Rumpers

Mrs Swabb (*announcing*) Delia, Lady Rumpers.

Lady Rumpers Felicity!

CURTAIN

ACT II

The same. Immediately following

Mrs Wicksteed We were just going to have a glass of sherry.
Lady Rumpers So I see.
Wicksteed You are Felicity's mother?
Lady Rumpers I am.

Lady Rumpers looks fixedly at Purdue who is still swinging

Wicksteed Take no notice. Some people will do anything for effect.

Wicksteed swings Purdue on to a chair where he stands with his head still in the noose

Purdue I don't really want to commit suicide. It's just a call for help.
Lady Rumpers So. I see I got here in the nick of time. Felicity, put that young man's hand back where it belongs and get some clothes on.
Felicity Yes, Mother.

Felicity exits

Lady Rumpers Who is that depressing youth?
Wicksteed My son. He depresses me, too.
Lady Rumpers Not too depressed to take my daughter's clothes off.
Wicksteed No, you worm.
Mrs Wicksteed He didn't.
Wicksteed Take no notice of my wife. She is his mother.
Lady Rumpers And you are his father.
Wicksteed Don't remind me.
Sir Percy Wicksteed did it. He is the culprit.
Wicksteed Yes. Yes. I did it. I am his father. I turned him into this, this snivelling, loathsome, little lecher. Where did I go wrong, where do we go wrong, we parents, generation after generation?
Sir Percy It's all lies. I can tell you what happened. I don't believe we've had the pleasure.
Mrs Swabb Allow me. This is Delia, Lady Rumpers.
Sir Percy Another titled person. What a breath of fresh air. Lady Rumpers, I am a doctor.
Lady Rumpers Another doctor. Then I don't want to hear another word. I've had a bellyful of doctors.
Purdue I want a doctor: I'm depressed.
Mrs Wicksteed So would I be if I had my head in a noose.
Purdue I only want to put *one* foot in the grave.

Lady Rumpers Oh, this is intolerable. Felicity. It shouldn't take all day for you to get your skirt on.
Wicksteed Can I help?
Lady Rumpers Don't touch her.

Dennis moves towards Felicity's position off stage

Wicksteed (*to Dennis*) No, get back. You've done enough damage already.
Dennis Me?
Wicksteed Control yourself.
Lady Rumpers Daring so much as even to look at a girl like Felicity.
Wicksteed Yes.
Mrs Wicksteed No.
Lady Rumpers You are dirt.
Wicksteed Dirt.
Lady Rumpers Filth.
Wicksteed Filth.

Felicity enters

Felicity Mother. He's sick.
Wicksteed Yes, sick; sick, sick. You toad.
Sir Percy If you'd allow me——
Wicksteed Shut your face.
Dennis Dad. Dad.
Wicksteed Don't "Dad, Dad" me.
Lady Rumpers To think we've only been in this country three weeks. Everywhere it's the same. Sex, sex, sex. Well I'm not having any.
Mrs Swabb I'm not surprised.
Lady Rumpers When I get you back to our suite at the Claremont, you're going straight into a hot bath and I shall personally scrub you all over with carbolic.
Wicksteed Ah, the privileges of motherhood.
Lady Rumpers Perhaps you will believe me now, Felicity. Men will touch you, rob you, rifle you of all you possess.
Sir Percy Flesh isn't property, you know.
Lady Rumpers Yes it is. What is one's body but property? What is one's own flesh and figure but the most precious inheritance? When that is spent one is indeed bankrupt of everything. From this moment on I shall not let her out of my sight. Haile Selassie was right. We should never have left Addis Ababa.

Lady Rumpers and Felicity exit

Mrs Wicksteed You slid out of that very well.

Dennis exits

Wicksteed I did rather.

Mrs Wicksteed I want you out of this house in half an hour.
Wicksteed Yes. I must collect my thoughts and pack.

Wicksteed exits

Mrs Wicksteed And we must have a little talk, Percy. About the future.
Sir Percy Yes.
Mrs Wicksteed Our future.

Sir Percy and Mrs Wicksteed exit

Purdue Has everybody gone?
Mrs Swabb Everybody of any consequence, dear.
Purdue Marvellous!
Mrs Swabb It's all self, self, self in this house. Locked in our tiny domestic tragedies only I, Amelia Swabb, can take the wider view. What seems to be the trouble?
Purdue I'm depressed.
Mrs Swabb Pisces is in the second quarter of Saturn: naturally you're depressed.
Purdue (*getting down*) I am Pisces.
Mrs Swabb Why don't you look on the bright side? Next week the Sun'll be in Saturn and Pisceans will be laughing.

Purdue and Mrs Swabb exit. Mrs Wicksteed and Sir Percy enter from the opposite side

Sir Percy I have no sympathy with him at all. None.
Mrs Wicksteed He *is* my husband.
Sir Percy I do not understand how he could betray such a fine body . . .
Mrs Wicksteed Nor do I.
Sir Percy As the British Medical Association.
Mrs Wicksteed What more does he want?

Wicksteed enters

Wicksteed Not more. Different.

Wicksteed exits

Sir Percy And a doctor. Entrusted with the bodies of his patients. Caught red-handed.
Mrs Wicksteed Red-handed, and yours so plump and white.
Sir Percy Please, Muriel. Of course we have all been tempted. Every doctor has. The lowliest locum in the back streets of Liverpool can take advantage of a patient, if he allows himself. Because the doctor-patient relationship is itself a kind of seduction. But one says, "No. No, body, I will not do this. No, hands, keep to your appointed task. No, eyes, stick to the affected part." That is what Professionalism means. Yes?

Mrs Wicksteed Have you . . .

Sir Percy Never, NEVER! Though I've had my chances. Discerning women seem to find me attractive, God knows why . . .

Mrs Wicksteed Yes.

Sir Percy Look, Muriel, there's something I have to tell you.

Mrs Wicksteed Yes?

Sir Percy Walk tall, Percy. This afternoon—I met the woman of my dreams.

Throbbing enters

Mrs Wicksteed Oh Percy. (*She kisses him*)

Throbbing Good evening.

Mrs Wicksteed Canon Throbbing! I want you to be the first to know, Arthur apart. And it will be Arthur apart. Separation City, I'm afraid. You must congratulate us.

Throbbing You and him? I think you must be mistaken. This man is engaged to my fiancée, Miss Wicksteed.

Mrs Wicksteed No, you are mistaken. You are engaged to your fiancée, Miss Wicksteed.

Throbbing That's what I thought until this afternoon.

Mrs Wicksteed This afternoon. What happened this afternoon?

Throbbing I was present when he proposed.

Mrs Wicksteed Percy and Connie?

Throbbing *He* proposed. She accepted. I protested. Then I had to get my skates on for Evensong.

Wicksteed enters

Wicksteed Evensong on ice? The Church must be desperate.

Wicksteed exits

Mrs Wicksteed Percy. Are you or are you not engaged to my sister-in-law?

Sir Percy Is your sister-in-law a woman with a nondescript face, but an outstanding figure?

Mrs Wicksteed Certainly not. She has a bust like a billiard table.

Throbbing She is as slim and graceful as a boy. Perhaps that is what attracted me to her in the first place.

Wicksteed enters

Wicksteed Sometimes I think Freud died in vain.

Wicksteed exits

Sir Percy Certainly a person purporting to be Miss Wicksteed thrust herself on me this afternoon. I can still feel her urgent young body rippling beneath my fingers.

Mrs Wicksteed It's unlike Connie to thrust herself, even slightly.

Throbbing He must have led her on.

Sir Percy It's animal magic.

Throbbing It's being little. They have to assert themselves.

Sir Percy Watch it, Vicar I gave your sister-in-law no encouragement at all.

Throbbing Then kindly explain, Lofty, how you came to be without your trousers.

Mrs Wicksteed Percy. Is this true?

Sir Percy No. Yes. President of the B.M.A., physician to the Queen: I can have any girl I want.

Mrs Wicksteed Connie! Come here this minute.

Connie enters, but without her appliance

Connie Yes, Muriel?

Mrs Wicksteed Don't Muriel me, you minx. You seem to have been busy this afternoon. Now, Percy. Is this the lady?

Sir Percy In some respects, yes. But what has happened to her urgent young body? I have been deceived. Terribly deceived. I don't want her either.

Mrs Wicksteed Now, Connie. Perhaps you can throw some light on the proceedings. Canon Thing here has got it into his head that you are all washed up. Is this true?

Connie Yes.

Throbbing No. Oh Mowgli, my wild jungle child, say it's not true.

Connie It is true.

Mrs Wicksteed Then who are you engaged to?

Connie To this gentleman here. He proposed to me.

Sir Percy Lies. LIES, LIES, ALL LIES!

Mrs Wicksteed Are you sure he proposed?

Connie Quite sure: he took his trousers off.

Sir Percy May I speak? MAY I SPEAK?

Mrs Wicksteed Percy.

Sir Percy MAY I?

Throbbing No.

Sir Percy Look here. I am Sir Percy Shorter, F.R.C.S., F.R.C.P.

Connie How do you do. I'm sure we're going to be very happy.

Sir Percy We are not. WE ARE NOT! WE ARE NOT GOING TO BE HAPPY AT ALL! I deny it. I deny everything. And I will go on denying everything. You believe her? Her unsupported—and I mean unsupported—word against mine. And you, Muriel. Think of the times we've had together. Do they mean nothing to you? NOTHING? This cringeing, flat-chested, dowdy little spinster. I am not going to throw myself away on that. It's all fantasy. A fantasy of frustration and loneliness and sadness and despair. And as such entirely DE-SPICABLE! I think you owe me an apology.

Mrs Wicksteed Percy. How could I have ever doubted your word.
Sir Percy And do you agree her talk was fantasy?
Mrs Wicksteed A tissue of lies.
Sir Percy Very well. I am big enough to overlook it.
Throbbing Just one moment. Am I right in thinking you deny anything
    untoward occurred this afternoon?
Sir Percy Absolutely. Absolutely.
Throbbing What time did you come here this afternoon?

The next sequence must be like a cross-examination, very gentle and slow,
then gradually increasing in speed leading to the fatal slip of the tongue

Sir Percy About three.
Throbbing About three?
Sir Percy About three.
Throbbing About three. You came into this room?
Sir Percy I came into this room.
Throbbing You're sure of that?
Sir Percy Of course I'm sure. Look here . . .
Throbbing Miss Wicksteed came in?
Sir Percy That is correct.
Throbbing And you say you arrived about three?
Sir Percy That is correct.
Throbbing And then you—what—talked?
Sir Percy Talked, chatted, made conversation.
Throbbing She was wearing a blue dress, is that right?
Sir Percy That is correct.
Throbbing So you arrived about three, came into this room, talked, chat-
    ted, made conversation . . .
Sir Percy Talked, chatted, made conversation . . .
Throbbing And she was wearing a blue dress?
Sir Percy A blue dress.
Throbbing She sat on the sofa?
Sir Percy She sat on the sofa.
Throbbing You stood?
Sir Percy That is correct.
Throbbing And you say you arrived about three? And came into this
    room?
Sir Percy Arrived about three, came into this room.
Throbbing Talked, chatted, made conversation?
Sir Percy Talked, chatted, made conversation.
Throbbing And she was in her blue dress?
Sir Percy And she was in her blue dress.
Throbbing And what colour were her knickers?
Sir Percy Green—no pink. Argh!
Throbbing Thank you, Sir Percy. That's all I wanted to know. I'm sorry,
    Miss Wicksteed. Your witness.
Mrs Wicksteed So. You big story.
Sir Percy Muriel.

Mrs Wicksteed Don't Muriel me, you four-foot Casanova.

Sir Percy You see, you see. It always has to come back to that.

Mrs Wicksteed All those years I've dreamed of you, the man I might have married.

Sir Percy All right, I wanted you once, but you spurned me and why? Because I was small. And your husband laughed. Well when I've finished with you you'll both be laughing on the other side of your faces. Little, small. So I'm small, am I? Well I'll tell you something, Muriel. You are not small. Not small at all. You are HUGE! ENORMOUS!

Mrs Wicksteed Stop it.

Sir Percy You think I fancied you? You!

Mrs Wicksteed You did, you did.

Sir Percy You great wardrobe. That model went out years ago.

Mrs Wicksteed Stop it. I'm ageless, do you hear, ageless!

Sir Percy And don't think you're going to trundle back to your snivelling little husband, and live happily ever after in your nice little provincial backwater. Because I am going to break him. BREAK HIM, do you hear? I've broken bigger men than that. And I'll do it again. Professional misconduct. Professional incompetence, interfering with patients—a list of charges as long as my arm.

Throbbing Well that's not very long.

Sir Percy Watch it, Vicar.

Connie Please don't do it. For my sake.

Sir Percy For your sake? What did you ever do for me, except pull the wool over my eyes?

Connie It was nice while it lasted.

Sir Percy It was an illusion.

Connie It always is.

Sir Percy No. I shall break him. He's had his chips.

Mrs Wicksteed No. No.

Sir Percy The party's over, Doctor. Curtains. This is the end of the line for you, Arthur Wicksteed, a general practitioner from Brighton's Hove.

Mrs Wicksteed The shame! The disgrace! The POVERTY!

Sir Percy *Finita La Commedia, Arturo.*

Sir Percy exits, followed by Mrs Wicksteed

Connie So you see now, marriage is out of the question.

Throbbing Is it?

Connie Oh yes. What I have done, you can't forgive. This foul, foul thing.

Throbbing It was only kissing.

Connie No. One kiss and he could have had anything. It would always lie between us. No, I am Damaged Goods.

Throbbing I forgive you.

Connie You mustn't. He mustn't.

Throbbing I must. It is my principles.

Connie I am a harlot. A Jezebel.

Throbbing I know, I know.

Connie A whore.

Throbbing Oh Connie, how infinitely more desirable you are now. Can't you see, Connie, what vistas are opening up?

Connie I think I can. Oh God.

Throbbing Sin with him you can sin with me. I wanted you before. I want you twice as much now.

Connie No, please, Harold, no.

Throbbing Gently we can lead each other on as together we explore all the alleys and pathways of the body. Just think of it.

Connie I'm trying not to.

Throbbing Together we shall be in the forefront of Anglican sexuality. Perhaps I might even write a frank and fearless account of our activities for the *Church Times*. Oh, such sin. Only it won't be sin because we shall be married, married and allowed to do what we want. Married and FREE!

Connie Free?

Throbbing (*to the tune of "Shuffle off to Buffalo"*)
  I must go and tell the verger
  That there'll shortly be a merger
  And it's some day soon.

Connie No, no, no.

Throbbing Can't believe my luck
  Because I'm going to break my duck
  Upon a honey, honey, honeymoon.

Connie and Throbbing exit, as Mrs Wicksteed and Mrs Swabb enter

Mrs Swabb It's kiss 'n' make up time. I'm glad to see somebody's doing the sensible thing.

Mrs Swabb exits

Mrs Wicksteed Now, Muriel old girl. You're going to have to play your cards pretty carefully, or you will end up on the discard pile. I don't know. And me with the menopause just shoving its nose above the horizon. As if I didn't have enough on my plate.

Wicksteed enters with his bags packed

Wicksteed I fold up my twenty-five years in the medical profession. I put in twenty-odd years of marriage, plus a slightly threadbare respectability. And that's it. All in ten minutes. Ten minutes and the world turns. Our world. In Memphis, Tennessee, fourteen babies have been born since this play began. In Hobart, Tasmania, a flower turns to the sun. In Lima, Peru, an old man is dying, and in Birmingham, England, two lovers turn to each other in the silence of the night—and somewhere out there in the singing silence of space, a tin flag flutters. Our world. Somewhere between the loving and the lying and the kissing and the crying and the living and the dying and the fishing and the frying is that something we call life. Our world.

Mrs Wicksteed All packed, I see.

Wicksteed A few things I've thrown together.

Mrs Wicksteed Where are you going?

Wicksteed Relatives.

Mrs Wicksteed Close relatives?

Wicksteed Stevenage. I think I have an aunt there.

Mrs Wicksteed You're a stinker, Arthur Wicksteed. Do you know that?

Wicksteed Oh yes.

Mrs Wicksteed A rotter.

Wicksteed It's funny. Having you, I didn't want you. Losing you, I want you again.

Mrs Wicksteed Hard cheese.

Wicksteed "His wife has promised to stand by him."

Mrs Wicksteed What?

Wicksteed I was just thinking, it would look better if you stood by me. Maybe I wouldn't be struck off.

Mrs Wicksteed It would *look* better. Of course I should have to dress the part: one thing I've learned in life is that few right-thinking people can withstand a really good twin-set and pearls. But what about my feelings?

Wicksteed I was forgetting those.

Mrs Wicksteed As usual. After all she wasn't just something on the side, was she? There've been others.

Wicksteed A few.

Mrs Wicksteed A few?

Wicksteed Quite a few.

Mrs Wicksteed I am fed up.

Wicksteed I think I am, too. Muriel. I suppose it's too late to start again.

Mrs Wicksteed Much too late. All those women lie between us.

Wicksteed And in your life, no-one?

Mrs Wicksteed No-one. Nothing. Never.

Wicksteed Percy?

Mrs Wicksteed A dream. A fantasy. No-one has ever laid a finger on me except you. And you it's so long, I've almost forgotten. Suppose I were to overlook your disgraceful conduct.

Wicksteed My shameful, shameful conduct. Filthy conduct.

Mrs Wicksteed Yes?

Wicksteed If only you could be big enough.

Mrs Wicksteed Then there'd have to be a different going on.

Wicksteed How different?

Mrs Wicksteed No more twin beds.

Wicksteed I sleep so badly.

Mrs Wicksteed Then we shall sleep badly together.

Wicksteed Yes, Muriel.

Mrs Wicksteed Perhaps in the long watches of the night I shall bring you comfort.

Wicksteed Perhaps you will.

Mrs Wicksteed I will. There is no perhaps about it. You see, you have no rights, Arthur. They have been forfeited over the years. Whereas innocence has kept mine intact. Kiss me.

Wicksteed Here?

Mrs Wicksteed Yes. No. Hard.

Wicksteed If you insist.

Wicksteed puts his arms around her and kisses her

Mrs Wicksteed And that's how it's going to be. But I am not forcing you. You may take it or leave it.

Wicksteed This or my aunt in Stevenage. I suppose I'd better take it.

Mrs Wicksteed A wise decision. Now I think we might retire for a little nap.

Wicksteed But I'm not tired.

Mrs Wicksteed Excellent. Neither am I.

Wicksteed Muriel. I . . .

Mrs Wicksteed What?

Wicksteed Nothing.

Mrs Wicksteed You see, innocence will always triumph in the end.

Wicksteed Though if there was anybody I'd forgive you. I know.

Mrs Wicksteed No need. There was nobody. Nobody at all. Now, what were we talking about? The future.

Wicksteed No. The past.

Mrs Wicksteed Then we must listen to the voice of the future.

Shanks enters

Shanks Has anybody seen my trousers?

Wicksteed Who is this?

Mrs Wicksteed Probably a patient left over from surgery.

Wicksteed He is not my patient.

Shanks I'm not anybody's patient.

Mrs Wicksteed Then you've no business here. Get out.

Shanks You again. No. Please don't touch me. No. No. Keep off!

Wicksteed Odd. He seems to know you.

Mrs Wicksteed In my voluntary work I rub shoulders with all sorts . . .

Shanks Don't let her touch me. You'll protect me, won't you?

Wicksteed Against what?

Shanks Against her.

Mrs Wicksteed I don't want to touch you.

Shanks You did before.

Mrs Wicksteed Hold your tongue.

Wicksteed Before? Before what, Muriel?

Mrs Wicksteed I don't know. How am I supposed to know?

Shanks She's a monster.

Wicksteed She is not a monster. She is my wife.

Shanks She's sex mad.

Mrs Wicksteed Listen, I wear the corsets in this house, so shut your cake-hole, before I give you a bunch of fives.

Wicksteed Muriel. Is there something between you and this man?

Mrs Wicksteed Arthur. I am not friends if you say things like that. It's quite plainly a delusion.

Shanks A delusion? Is this a delusion? (*He shows Wicksteed the Polaroid snaps*) Or this? The camera cannot lie.

Wicksteed What wonderful pictures. Who is it?

Shanks Who? It's her.

Wicksteed Good God. So it is. Muriel, what have you got to say?

Mrs Wicksteed Damn. Damn. I am ruined.

Wicksteed Is this your clear conscience? *Qu'est-ce que c'est que ça, madame?* Not to mention *que ça.*

Mrs Wicksteed Silliness, silliness. That was all it was.

Wicksteed Is this your innocence? (*He plucks at Shanks's shirt-tails*) Or this?

Shanks Stop it.

Wicksteed So. Now it's my turn.

Mrs Wicksteed No. Arthur, please.

Wicksteed Don't touch me. Don't touch me. You're not fit to touch me.

Mrs Wicksteed It was a mistake.

Wicksteed And don't grovel. I can't abide a groveller. You see, I always thought no-one else fancied her. I've always had this sneaking feeling that if I hadn't married her, no-one else would. But—(*he looks at the snaps*)—my goodness me! It's *Forever Amber* all over again. Flower arrangements, cake decorating. All those long suburban afternoons . . . It was lovers, lovers from all walks of life, like you. How long has this been going on?

Mrs Wicksteed This afternoon. Ten minutes. That's all.

Wicksteed I don't believe it. I believe it's been going on for years. Sex isn't something that happens overnight, you know.

Mrs Wicksteed You're wrong, so wrong. (*She moves away*)

Wicksteed Go to your room. Pack one or two things, just in case. You may have to go to your mother's. (*To Shanks*) And you, get out!

Shanks I'd like to ex——

Wicksteed Get out!

Shanks exits

Mrs Wicksteed (*returning*) Arthur.

Wicksteed Yes.

Mrs Wicksteed Am I to be turned out of my own house?

Wicksteed I was.

Mrs Wicksteed Can't we forgive and forget? We can live on our memories.

Wicksteed I have no memories, only scars.

Mrs Wicksteed Arthur, please.
Wicksteed No, Muriel.

Mrs Wicksteed exits

Wicksteed The eyes, cool but kindly, looked back unflinchingly from the glass. There was pain in those eyes, a hint perhaps of some secret sorrow. He ran his lean brown fingers through his thinning hair and sighed. And yet, at the corner of his firm, yet sensitive mouth, there hovered the merest suspicion of a smile. "I'm still in the game" he thought.

Wicksteed exits. Shanks and Mrs Swabb enter

Mrs Swabb I see you're still in your underpants. And the same pair, too. Have you never heard of the dictum: undies worn twice are not quite nice?
Shanks No.

Shanks exits

Mrs Swabb And they talk of comprehensive education.

Purdue enters

Purdue That is the dirtiest gas oven I've ever put my head in.
Mrs Swabb It's not gas, it's electric.

Mrs Swabb exits. Felicity and Dennis enter

Dennis Felicity.
Felicity I gave her the slip. I had to see you again.
Dennis Yes. I feel the same way. Except . . .
Felicity Except what?
Dennis Could you love me if I wasn't going to die?
Felicity But you are.
Dennis I mean we all die sooner or later. So say it was later rather than sooner.
Felicity How much later?
Dennis Round about the time you're supposed to die, three score years and ten.
Felicity How much is that?
Dennis Seventy.
Felicity Another fifty years. No, my love, we must resign ourselves, there is no hope.
Dennis No. I don't think there is.

Shanks enters

Shanks At last.

Mrs Swabb enters

Mrs Swabb Oh no. Not again.

Mrs Swabb exits

Shanks approaches Felicity

Shanks I had rather an unpleasant experience earlier, so you'll forgive me if I'm cautious.
Felicity How do you do.
Shanks I thought I must be losing my touch. But no. One look at you and I realize, those could never be real.

Mrs Swabb, Dr and Mrs Wicksteed, Canon Throbbing and Connie come on and watch, fascinated

Shanks The line so crisp, the silhouette so pert. If that's not our product I'll go back to chicken farming.

He touches Felicity's breast and she slaps his face

Mrs Wicksteed I second that. (*She fetches Shanks another slap*)
Shanks I can't understand it. On the training course they teach you to tell blindfold.
Wicksteed What are you doing here, anyway?
Shanks I'm looking for my client.

Felicity slaps him again

Dennis Without your trousers?
Throbbing Is he a commercial traveller?

Connie slaps Throbbing

Shanks In a sense.
Dennis If he's a commercial traveller, he must often be without his trousers.

Wicksteed slaps Dennis

Mrs Wicksteed Arthur!
Throbbing What do you travel in?

Connie slaps Throbbing, Mrs Wicksteed slaps Wicksteed, Shanks slaps Dennis, Wicksteed slaps Mrs Wicksteed

Lady Rumpers enters

Mrs Swabb Delia, Lady Rumpers.
Lady Rumpers Out of my way, you pert slut. Is this what we were promised

when we emerged from the Dark Ages? Is this Civilization? I'm only
thankful Kenneth Clark isn't here to see it.
Mrs Swabb I'm not actually sure he isn't.

Mrs Swabb exits

Lady Rumpers (*to Shanks*) You.
Shanks Good evening.
Lady Rumpers Good evening. What has happened to your trousers?
Shanks I don't know.
Lady Rumpers Well you'd better find them. If I'd wanted to see people
running about in their shirt-tails I should have stayed in Addis Ababa.

Shanks exits

Connie Good evening.
Lady Rumpers Good evening.
Throbbing Good evening.
Lady Rumpers Good evening. Why should your face be familiar? Have
you ever been called to serve the Lord in heathen parts?
Throbbing Well, I was for a short time a curate in Leeds.
Mrs Wicksteed Good evening.
Wicksteed Good evening.
Lady Rumpers All in all I can say quite confidently I have seen nothing like
this even in the cesspots of Mespot. And, Felicity, leave that dismal boy
alone.
Wicksteed Hear, hear.
Lady Rumpers Shut up. Do you hear?
Felicity No. I won't. I love Dennis.
Dennis We want to get married.
Lady Rumpers Love, madam. I do not want to hear that word. You talk
of love with a body like yours. Time enough to fall back on love when
the bloom begins to fade. I didn't slave away bringing you up in a
temperature of a hundred and fifteen in the shade for you to talk of
love as soon as my back is turned.
Wicksteed I quite agree.
Lady Rumpers Shut up.
Mrs Wicksteed Hear, hear.
Lady Rumpers You too. The word marriage has been mentioned. It is
out of the question. Felicity is far too young for a start . . .
Felicity But Mother . . .
Lady Rumpers And the young man——
Wicksteed Keith.
Mrs Wicksteed Dennis.
Wicksteed Trevor, yes.
Lady Rumpers —far too ugly.
Wicksteed True. A boy like that proposing marriage to a girl the strap
of whose bra he is not worthy to undo.

Lady Rumpers Don't touch her.

Wicksteed Don't touch her.

Throbbing Could I say something?

Lady Rumpers ⎫
Connie ⎭ No. { (*Speaking together*)

Mrs Wicksteed May a mother have a voice?

Lady Rumpers ⎫
Wicksteed ⎭ No. { (*Speaking together*)

Lady Rumpers A girl like Felicity and a shrivelled thing like him. Think of the stock. Why, you wouldn't do it to a hyacinth.

Mrs Wicksteed Hyacinths don't fall in love.

Wicksteed If you ask me, he wants a kick up the arse.

Lady Rumpers Come, Felicity. It's time we were going. When I hear the word arse I know the way the wind is blowing.

Mrs Wicksteed Lady Rumpers. Arthur. One moment. Fair do's. We're all of us pretty well headed for the sere and yellow. It's times hurrying footsteps all round these days, isn't it? Now, Dennis, he's not a glamour puss. Never will be. Even though he is the fruit of our loins. Partly our fault. Funny boy. Difficult to love. Never liked touching him very much and quite frankly it makes a difference. Touching, looking, loving— without it which one of us would thrive? Look at your girl, Felicity. Stroked and cherished all her life. Lovely girl.

Lady Rumpers Lovely girl.

Wicksteed Lovely girl.

Mrs Wicksteed But that's because she's been worn next to the heart. Result: she blooms. Dennis, shoved away at the back of the drawer, result: drab, boring, spotty, nobody wants him.

Connie But that's me, too.

Mrs Swabb enters

Mrs Wicksteed But I say this: love him, as your girl seems unaccountably to love him, and he'll blossom.

Mrs Swabb I think he's looking better already.

Lady Rumpers No, never. It's quite right you should be kind to him. You are his mother. I am under no such handicap.

Connie Please.

Lady Rumpers No.

Mrs Swabb Please.

Lady Rumpers No.

Dennis Please.

Lady Rumpers No.

Felicity Please.

Lady Rumpers No. My daughter . . .

Wicksteed Oh, stuff your daughter.

Mrs Swabb (*indicating Dennis*) He already has.

Lady Rumpers What?

Lady Rumpers gives a great cry, and swoons

Mrs Swabb Did I strike a wrong note?

Wicksteed Excuse me, I'm a doctor.

Mrs Wicksteed We know you're a doctor.

Wicksteed She has fainted.

Mrs Wicksteed Dennis, is this true?

Mrs Swabb Quite true. Between fifteen-ten and fifteen-twenty-five this afternoon they carried out the docking procedure.

Wicksteed You mean, you and her, her and you?

Dennis Yes.

Throbbing What was it like?

Lady Rumpers After all my precautions. Gone. Tossed away on him.

Felicity No. It was love.

Lady Rumpers Love. You don't understand. No-one understands. The shame. The waste. My own shameful story all over again.

Mrs Wicksteed Oh crumbs!

Lady Rumpers Many years ago, when I was not much older than Felicity is now, I had just arrived in the colonies. I—you have to know this, Felicity. I should have told you before. I had just arrived in the colonies when I found I was P-R-E-G-N-A-N-T.

Throbbing PRAGNENT?

Mrs Wicksteed Pegnat.

Lady Rumpers PREGNANT! I was not married at the time.

Mrs Wicksteed What about General Rumpers?

Lady Rumpers Tiger and I met soon afterwards. He loved me. I—respected him. We married. He was a gentleman but shy. He only went into the Army in order to put his moustache to good purpose. He was glad of a child for his life too had its secrets: a passing-out party at Sandhurst had left him forever incapable of having children. He threw the blanket of his name over Felicity and together we achieved respectability. Call me fool, call me slut, call me anything you like. But I vowed at that time that the same thing should never happen to Felicity. And now it has. My poor child. Oh Felicity, Felicity.

Wicksteed And where is he now, her real father?

Lady Rumpers Do you think I have not asked myself that question? Lying under mosquito nets in Government House; do you think that question has not hammered itself into my brain?

Wicksteed Have you any clues?

Lady Rumpers One and one only. He was a doctor. Yes. That is why I despise your profession.

Mrs Wicksteed His name. Do you know that?

Lady Rumpers No. I suppose that shocks you.

Mrs Wicksteed Nothing could shock me any more.

Lady Rumpers Picture the scene. Liverpool. The blitz at its height. I am bound for the Far East. Our convoy is assembled ready to go down the Mersey on the morning tide. Suddenly I am told I cannot sail.

Wicksteed Yes?

Lady Rumpers No. I had no vaccination certificate. The black-out. An air-raid in progress. The docks ablaze. I set off alone to find a doctor.

Buildings crashing all round me. Crash, crash, crash. Bombs raining down on the street. Boom, boom, boom. I see a brass plate. The surgery in darkness. The doctor under the table. He writes me a certificate. I am grateful. Think how grateful I was. We talk.

Throbbing Yes, yes, go on.

Lady Rumpers Two voices in the darkness of the surgery as the storm rages outside. His hand steals into mine . . .

Throbbing Yes, then what did he do?

Lady Rumpers We cling to each other as the bombs fell.

Throbbing Yes?

Lady Rumpers I need not tell you the rest.

Throbbing They always miss out the best bits.

Lady Rumpers The "all clear" sounds as I stumble back on board. Came the dawn we slipped out of the Mersey and headed for the open sea. Do you know the Atlantic at all?

Mrs Wicksteed No.

Lady Rumpers It is very rough. I thought I was sea sick. Only when we docked did I realize I had a bun in the club.

Mrs Wicksteed Tragic.

Wicksteed Wonderful.

Lady Rumpers I blame the War.

Wicksteed Ah the War, that was a strange and wonderful time.
 Oh Mavis and Audrey and Lilian and Jean
 Patricia and Pauline and NAAFI Christine
 Maureen and Myrtle I had you and more
 In God's gift to the lecher the Second World War.

Mrs Swabb In shelters and bunkers on Nissen hut floors,
 They wrestled with webbing and cellular drawers.
 From pillbox on headland they scoured the seas
 While pinching our bottoms and stroking our knees.

Lady Rumpers Echoes of music drift into the night.
 Never in peace will it all seem so right.

Wicksteed Oh Lost Generation, where are you now?
 I still see Lemira, Yvonne's in Slough.
 Mothers like you, with girls in their twenties.
 Fathers like me: we all share such memories.

Lady Rumpers One mad magenta moment and I have paid for it all my life. Felicity ruined.

Connie and Throbbing exit

Mrs Swabb We don't know she is, do we? One swallow doesn't make a summer.

Felicity Never mind, Mummy. After all he wants to marry me.

Lady Rumpers Yes. Go, Felicity. Be happy.

Felicity Happy. Oh Mummy, if you only knew.

Wicksteed Such a waste.

Mrs Wicksteed At least somebody's happy.

Wicksteed Is she happy?

Mrs Swabb She looks happy to me. But then I'm a behaviourist.

Mrs Wicksteed You're a busybody.

Mrs Swabb And I can make her happier still.

Felicity Nobody can make me happier.

Mrs Swabb I can. I want to explain about Dennis.

Dennis No, Mrs Swabb, no.

Felicity Such a short time we have together.

Mrs Swabb But it isn't.

Felicity It's three months.

Mrs Swabb No.

Felicity No?

Dennis No.

Felicity Longer?

Mrs Swabb Yes.

Dennis No.

Felicity Much longer?

Mrs Swabb Much, much longer.

Felicity Much, much longer.

Felicity You mean . . . he's not going to die at all?

Mrs Swabb Strong as a horse.

Dennis
Felicity } Oh, no. { *(Speaking together)*

Felicity and Dennis exit

Mrs Swabb It's all in the mind.

Wicksteed This doctor in Liverpool, I'm interested. What did he look like?

Lady Rumpers As I say there was a black-out. I saw his face only in the fitful light of a post-coital Craven A. He was small, but perfectly proportioned. In some respects more so. I don't suppose I shall ever find him.

Mrs Swabb Who knows. One day the doorbell will go and he will walk back into her life again.

The doorbell rings

Throbbing enters

Throbbing Isn't that the doorbell?

Throbbing exits

Wicksteed Don't let's jump to conclusions. It could be the man next door taking his first tentative steps on the xylophone.

Sir Percy enters

Mrs Swabb Sir Percy Shorter.

Mrs Swabb exits

Sir Percy I wish to speak to your daughter.

Lady Rumpers My daughter has been spoken to by at least four people this afternoon, one of whom has proposed marriage. Naturally, she is exhausted.

Sir Percy I wish to take down her evidence.

Mrs Wicksteed You've taken down quite enough this afternoon.

Sir Percy LIES, LIES!

Lady Rumpers What sort of evidence?

Sir Percy She has this very afternoon been assaulted.

Mrs Wicksteed Haven't we all.

Lady Rumpers Suffice it to say that my daughter is to marry the person who assaulted her.

Sir Percy But he is married already. To this lady. (*He indicates Mrs Wicksteed*)

Lady Rumpers Indeed. She has been masquerading as his mother. These are new depths.

Wicksteed Understandably, Sir Percy is a little confused.

Sir Percy Little!

Wicksteed He is over-excited. You are over-excited.

Sir Percy That is not true. I was never more calm in my life. I am the only person here telling the truth. Unclean, unclean. I'll break you. Under cover of a medical examination this man assaulted your daughter.

Lady Rumpers You? My daughter appears to have been assaulted by the whole family.

Mrs Wicksteed No. Not me.

Wicksteed No. Not you. You confined yourself to our friend in the shirt-tails. You're the prey of any tom-cat that knocks at the door.

Sir Percy (*to Wicksteed*) You can talk.

Mrs Wicksteed (*to Sir Percy*) You can talk.

Shanks enters

Shanks (*to Mrs Wicksteed*) You can talk.

Throbbing and Connie enter. Shanks, Sir Percy, Wicksteed and Mrs Wicksteed exit

Throbbing I seem to be the only one with nothing to be ashamed of.

Lady Rumpers Now I remember you. You are the Beast of the ten-twenty-six. Just because you're a clergyman you think you can look up girls' legs.

Lady Rumpers exits

Connie Is this true?
Throbbing One has to look somewhere.
Connie Harold! Don't touch me.

Throbbing and Connie exit. Felicity and Dennis enter

Felicity Don't touch me. Don't touch me.
Dennis Penelope.
Felicity FELICITY! I despise you. You lied to me.
Dennis Not really.
Felicity I thought it was only going to be for three months.
Dennis But you said you loved me.
Felicity All your faults . . . the stuff you put on your hair, your awful
    trousers, your terrible, terrible feet. For three months yes, I could swal-
    low it all, string vests, everything. But not for *life*!
Dennis What if I promised to commit suicide at the end of three months?
Felicity It's very nice of you, but it wouldn't be the same. Don't touch
    me.

Dennis and Felicity exit. Wicksteed, Mrs Wicksteed and Sir Percy enter

Mrs Wicksteed Arthur.
Wicksteed Don't touch me.

Felicity and Dennis enter

Felicity (*to Dennis*) Don't touch me.
Wicksteed (*to Sir Percy*) Don't touch me.

Connie and Throbbing enter

Connie (*to Throbbing*) Don't touch me.
Sir Percy All in all, I can say quite confidently that I've seen nothing like
    this since I was a locum in Liverpool.

All come on slowly, and stand in a great circle round Sir Percy

Mrs Swabb And now, suddenly the air is black with the wings of chickens
    coming home to roost.
Wicksteed You did say Liverpool?
Sir Percy Liverpool.
Lady Rumpers Liverpool?
Mrs Wicksteed Liverpool.
Mrs Swabb Liverpool.
Sir Percy Yes, Liverpool. What of it. I did a locum there. In the War.
Wicksteed Yes, of course, the War.
Lady Rumpers That would be the Second War, the one to make the world
    safe for democracy?

Sir Percy That was how it was advertised.

Wicksteed When the enemy was always listening, and cigarettes were two a penny. (*He lights a cigarette lighter*)

Mrs Swabb Put that light out.

Darkness, the sounds of an air-raid

Lady Rumpers That's him! That's him!

Sir Percy Who?

Lady Rumpers My seducer.

Sir Percy Are you all mad?

Wicksteed Liverpool. The War. The docks. Yes?

Sir Percy No.

Wicksteed Buildings crashing down. Whole streets ablaze. Yes?

Sir Percy No. No.

Wicksteed A doctor's surgery. Yes?

Sir Percy I don't remember.

Wicksteed Your surgery.

Sir Percy No.

Wicksteed And then, a knock comes at the door. It is a patient. A woman.

Sir Percy It could have been anybody.

Wicksteed But it wasn't anybody.

Sir Percy It was nobody.

Lady Rumpers Nobody! It was me!

The Lights come up

Sir Percy You!

Lady Rumpers Don't you remember how we clung to each other in the darkness of the surgery?

Throbbing Yes. Yes. Tell it like it is.

Sir Percy No.

Lady Rumpers And then you took me.

Throbbing Yee-ow.

Sir Percy I took *you*? You took *me*. Your Land Army breeches came down with a fluency born of long practice.

Lady Rumpers It is immaterial.

Throbbing Could we go back over that bit in more detail?

Sir Percy No.

Throbbing They've missed it out again.

Lady Rumpers There was a child. She lived and found powerful friends. She is living now. She is a lady and very beautiful.

Dennis And I love her.

Dennis exits

Felicity weeps

Sir Percy What's the matter with her?

Wicksteed It must be something of a shock to find she's got you for a father.

Sir Percy Father? Me? Bless her. To think, all these years denied the chance of lavishing on her fatherly affections. Those little services of love which are a father's right. Stroke her hair, wipe away her tears, bath her.

Lady Rumpers Bath her?

Sir Percy Well, perhaps no. But help her choose her dresses, rub on her suntan lotion . . . those one hundred and one things only a father can do. You can see she needs a father's hand.

Wicksteed Not down her blouse.

Lady Rumpers I see you haven't changed. No word of regret.

Sir Percy The incident had vanished from my mind.

Lady Rumpers You funny little man.

Sir Percy Don't say that.

Lady Rumpers Rumpers was a little man, too. He made no secret of his height. Strange, I've been looking for you all my life and now I've found you I don't know what to do with you.

Sir Percy You've got nothing to do with me.

Lady Rumpers You don't even seem sorry.

Sir Percy Why should I be sorry? I didn't know there was a child.

Wicksteed And are you in the habit of seducing every patient who comes into your surgery?

Sir Percy It was the War.

Wicksteed And Lady Rumpers was your patient?

Sir Percy No.

Lady Rumpers You were the doctor, I was the patient and Felicity was the outcome.

Lady Rumpers and Felicity exit

Wicksteed Tut, tut, tut. Hard lines, Perce.

Sir Percy Don't call me Perce. I am Sir Percy Shorter, President of the B.M.A.

Wicksteed Not for much longer.

Sir Percy You wouldn't dare.

Wicksteed I would. Unprofessional conduct. Interfering with patients. A list of charges as long as your arm, no, my arm. And the chief witness your own illegitimate daughter. I think it's sleeping dogs' time, Percy. Otherwise, one word and it's curtains, *finito*.

Sir Percy It's not fair. Why is it always me?

Wicksteed How extraordinary! So even you, Percy, are human. Just like the rest of us, the world over. Each one of us walking the world because someone somewhere happened to bring their body and lay it against another body. Everyone. Every person you see in the street, read about in the newspaper. All the names in the births' column. All the names in the deaths' column. Chinese swimming rivers with guns in their mouths, the Ryder Cup team. The Pope on his balcony. Everybody. Everywhere. All the time.

Wicksteed exits. Mrs Swabb enters

Mrs Swabb (*bowing deeply*) Sir Percy. Could I crave a boon?

Sir Percy She's mad, too. They're all in the plot.

Mrs Swabb Examine Dennis. Tell her he's dying. Pretend.

Sir Percy Pretend? Tell her, who? Why?

Mrs Swabb Felicity.

Sir Percy My daughter? Pretend? I couldn't pretend that. I couldn't. You don't know what you're asking. My position. Jeopardizing my professional integrity.

Mrs Swabb You haven't got any. Not now.

Sir Percy Nobody knows that.

Mrs Swabb They could always find out.

Sir Percy LIES! LIES! Blackmail. It's a PLOT! I WILL NEVER DO IT! NEVER, NEVER, NEVER! Where is he?

Mrs Swabb Follow me, Sir Percy. I will conduct you thither.

Mrs Swabb and Sir Percy exit hand in hand. Felicity and Connie, wearing her appliance, enter, each looking at themselves

Connie It used to be so flat.

Felicity It used to be so flat.

Connie Can you tell?

Felicity You can tell.

Shanks, in Purdue's trousers, comes upon Connie still trying to adjust her bust. They enter from opposite sides

Shanks Something tells me you're the person we're looking for. Miss Wicksteed?

Connie Yes.

Shanks Allow me. There. Striking without being indiscreet. Full but not vulgar. What a day. Would you like to take a walk?

Connie In the street? Won't people stare?

Shanks At a striking woman. Yes. People will stare.

Connie I shall need different clothes, a larger fit. My hair ought to be different. My whole style.

Shanks Come. The world is waiting.

Shanks and Connie exit. Sir Percy, Dennis and Mrs Swabb enter

Sir Percy There is no doubt about it. Brett's Palsy.

Mrs Swabb Brett's Palsy. How terrible. How terrible, Felicity.

Dennis Don't overdo it.

Sir Percy In it's tertiary stage.

Mrs Swabb Tertiary. That's good. Tertiary is good. Tertiary is very good.

Dennis How long have I got?

Sir Percy Do you really want me to tell you?

Dennis For the sake of my fiancée, yes.

Felicity Your former fiancée. I gave you back the ring.

Sir Percy In the circumstances a wise precaution. Your engagement would
have been broken off anyway.
Felicity You mean . . . ?
Sir Percy I'm afraid so. Three months. Four at the outside.
Felicity You're sure?
Mrs Swabb President of the B.M.A. Physician to the Queen, course he's
sure. A man in his position can't afford to make mistakes, can you?
Sir Percy No.
Felicity Oh Dennis. Forgive me.
Dennis So I do have Brett's Palsy after all. I knew I had Brett's Palsy.
I always said I had Brett's Palsy. Felicity, how could you ever have
doubted I had Brett's Palsy. Time is short. We must be married this
minute.

Dennis and Felicity exit

Mrs Swabb That was very sporting of you, Sir Percy.
Sir Percy Not difficult. Really rather sad.
Mrs Swabb Sad? Why?
Sir Percy He has three months to live. He thought he had Brett's Palsy.
He has got Brett's Palsy. As paranoids sometimes have enemies, so
hypochondriacs sometimes have diseases. It isn't always in the mind.
Mrs Swabb But he's so happy.
Sir Percy So what are you weeping about? He's happy. He's got his lady
love. She's happy. She thinks he's going to die. He is going to die.
Everybody's happy. Except me.

Sir Percy exits

Mrs Swabb Well we're into injury time now.
There's no time to make a rhyme up.
Just the wedding and the line-up

Wicksteed and Mrs Wicksteed enter

Mrs Wicksteed Dear Dennis, I hope he's making the right decision.
Wicksteed What does it matter? He's in love.
Mrs Wicksteed And we're back where we started.
Wicksteed I say love. That great conglomerate. Affection and attraction,
envy and desire. All marketed under the same label. A father's love, a
daughter's love, love of wives for husbands and mothers for children.
It's love all right. But which department—the headquarters in the heart
or the depot between the legs?
Mrs Wicksteed Do try not to be vulgar, Arthur, or we shall never get on.
Wicksteed Only time will tell.
Mrs Swabb Delia, Lady Rumpers.

Lady Rumpers enters

Lady Rumpers From youth and from desiring
    From love and passion free
    Old with too much regretting
    My future's plain to see.
    A small hotel in Eastbourne
    A nightly game of whist.
    An old colonial lady
    Who'll die and not be missed.

Sir Percy enters

Sir Percy But Delia, I too am lonely
    For lonely are the brave
    Come. Why do we not go together,
    In step towards the grave?

Sir Percy and Lady Rumpers exit

Mrs Swabb So as the shadows lengthen
    Across the lawns of life
    They walk into the sunset . . .
    Sir Percy and his wife.

Connie sweeps on, transformed, with Shanks

    These flashing legs
    This smile so regal.
    I know that face.
    Dame Anna Neagle!
Connie No, no. You fool. It's me, it's me.
    Got up like an awful tart,
    But ready now to pay to Life
    The debt I owe to Art.
    My new fiancé, Denzil here,
    Is keen on heavy petting
    He wants to go too far with me
    And by God I'm going to let him.

Throbbing enters

Throbbing (*to Connie*) Your future hopes, your married bliss
    On firm foundations rest.
    Who knows, one day, I just might be.
    A guest upon that breast.
    My life I squandered waiting
    Then let my chance go by.
    One day we'll meet in Heaven.
    That Matlock in the sky.

Mrs Swabb That's a refreshing change. The first time this evening everyone
has had their trousers on.

Purdue enters without trousers

I might have known. Where are your trousers?
Purdue I gave them to him. You don't need trousers where I'm going.
I've just taken fifty sleeping-pills. The pink ones.
Wicksteed Those aren't sleeping-pills. They're laxatives.

Purdue exits hurriedly

Mrs Swabb He's right. You don't need trousers where he's going.

Dennis and Felicity enter

Throbbing presides over the wedding of Dennis and Felicity

Dennis Yes, I take this woman.
    For my lawful wedded wife.
Felicity To honour, love and cherish.
    The remainder of his life.
Dennis It will be longer than she thinks.
Mrs Swabb And shorter than he knows.
Felicity My breast is filled with happiness.
Connie And mine with cellulose.

All dance

Mrs Swabb The body's an empty vessel,
    The flesh an awful cheat,
    The world is just an abattoir,
    For our rotting lumps of meat.
    So if you get your heart's desire,
    Your longings come to pass,
    Remember in each other's beds
    It isn't going to last.
    The smoothest cheek will wrinkle
    The proudest breast will fall.
    Some sooner go, some later
    But death will claim us all.
Wicksteed No, no, no. Well, yes—but . . .
Mrs Wicksteed But what?

During Wicksteed's speech everyone gradually exits, leaving him alone

Wicksteed But on those last afternoons in the bed by the door.
    On the Clement Attlee Ward,
    When you mourn the loss of energy

Even Lucozade cannot replace
And Sister Tudor thinks you may go any time
Do you think that you think
Of the things that you did
Or the things that you didn't do?
The promise broken, the meeting you missed,
The word not spoken, the cheek not kissed.
Lust was it or love? Was it false or true?
Who cares now?
Dying you'll grieve for what you didn't do.
The young are not the innocent, the old are not the wise,
Unless you've proved it for yourselves,
Morality is lies.
So this is my prescription: grab any chance you get
Because if you take it or you leave it,
You end up with regret.
Put it this way.
A Voice (*off*) Arthur.
Wicksteed Whatever right or wrong is
He whose lust lasts, lasts longest.

Wicksteed dances alone in the spotlight until he can dance no more, and—

the CURTAIN *falls*

FURNITURE AND PROPERTY LIST

ACT I

On stage: 3 chairs

Off stage: Vacuum cleaner **(Mrs Swabb)**
Power-assisted bicycle **(Throbbing)**
Medical book **(Dennis)**
Magazine with postcard **(Mrs Swabb)**
Telephone **(Wicksteed** and **others)**
Parcel containing **Connie's** "appliance" **(Mrs Swabb)**
Copy of the *Lancet* **(Mrs Swabb)**
Polaroid camera **(Shanks)**
Hypodermic syringe **(Mrs Wicksteed)**
Wheeled basket of groceries **(Mrs Swabb)**
Noosed rope **(Purdue)**

Personal: **Mrs Swabb:** pencil

ACT II

Off stage: Snapshots **(Shanks)**
2 suitcases **(Wicksteed)**

Personal: **Wicksteed:** cigarette lighter

'Hanging' Man Effect
The necessary equipment for this effect can be hired from Hi-Fli Ltd,
The Flying Effects Co., Grand Theatre, Wolverhampton.

LIGHTING PLOT

NOTE: The following plot includes only cues having a direct bearing on the action. Other following spots, etc., may be added at the producer's discretion

Property fittings required: nil
A bare stage. The same scene throughout

ACT I

To open: Single spot on **Wicksteed**, c

Cue 1	**Mrs Swabb:** ". . . the wonderful, wonderful Wicksteed family."	(Page 1)
	Bring up general lighting to full	
Cue 2	**Wicksteed:** ". . . show you a cesspit."	(Page 9)
	Bring up rose-coloured spot to cover **Felicity's** *entrance*	

ACT II

To open: As close of Act I

Cue 3	**Mrs Swabb:** "Put that light out."	(Page 51)
	Black-out	
Cue 4	**Lady Rumpers:** "Nobody! It was me!"	(Page 51)
	Lights up as before	
Cue 5	**Wicksteed:** "But on those last afternoons . . ."	(Page 56)
	Slow fade throughout speech to a single spot on **Wicksteed**	

EFFECTS PLOT

ACT I